PROGRAMS
for
Advent
and
Christmas

PROGRAMS FOR ADVENT AND CHRISTMAS

The programs, plays, pageants, and other Christmas ideas found herein were originally published in the October, 1976, October, 1977, and December, 1977, issues of *Baptist Leader*. All the programs were successfully used by churches across the country who have shared their experiences with us.

PHOTO CREDITS: pp. 4, 7, 34, 47, 53, 54 top, Camerique; pp. 9 bottom, 48, 54 bottom, 55 bottom, H. Armstrong Roberts; pp. 9 top, 12, 13, Jeffrey Jones; p. 10, Religious News Service; pp. 27, 28, Donald Johnson; p. 30, Robert Maust; pp. 31, 32, Paul M. Schrock; pp. 33, 35, 43, David S. Strickler; pp. 36, 37, 38, Thomas G. Bayes; pp. 39, 40, 41, Neal A. Koch.

PROGRAMS
for Advent and Christmas

Compiled and edited by Vincie Alessi

Judson Press ® Valley Forge

Contents

Hanging of the Greens and Carol Sing

From a service by H. Victor Kane
adapted by Nicholas Titus

PART I. *Outdoor Carol Sing*

While carols are sung informally on the porch of the church, the choir figures, the large star (above the outside door), and the rope of greens (around the outside door frame) are put in place.

(Possibility: Robed youth choir standing on inside steps leading to nave, leading the singing—with both front doors wide open.)

(Possibility: Outdoor crèche scene also put in place during the carol sing.)

PART II. *Hanging of the Greens and Indoor Carol Sing*

The youth choir shall lead the congregation as it proceeds down the aisle singing "O Come, All Ye Faithful."

Adapted from a service of H. Victor Kane by Nicholas Titus, when Mr. Titus was Executive Secretary of the Connecticut Baptist Convention. The *original* service by the Reverend Kane appeared in **Baptist Leader**, November, 1965. The adapted service was taken from *Worship Services for Special Occasions,* compiled and edited by Norman L. Hersey (The World Publishing Company © 1970).

Readers follow the choir and take their places behind the two desks.

SCRIPTURE READING

PRAYER

(Lights are dimmed.)

INTRODUCTION

Almost two thousand years ago, some simple shepherds were watching over their sheep on Judean hillsides in far-off Palestine. It was night . . . and it was very still.

Suddenly the darkness was filled with a strange light. The stillness was broken by the sound of angel voices singing: "Glory to God in the highest, and on earth peace, goodwill toward men." So began our most beautiful and meaningful religious festival—Christmas.

Christmas, like a great cathedral, has been developing through many centuries. It is still changing and continuing to grow, as old customs are refined and new traditions begin.

Christmas is celebrated in home and church. It's true some of our celebrations have their origin in pagan customs and have little to do with the biblical account of the birth of Christ. These have been brought to Christmas by the converts to Christianity.

We need have no qualms about using these customs—for the customs, along with the people, were converted to Christianity. These ancient celebrations are being laid at His feet, as gifts for the Christ Child. They can only enrich and gladden the heart of the believer, as he brings his own best before the newborn King in solemn dedication.

Tonight our church will begin to wear its Christmas apparel. We will change the appearance of the church, in order to make ready for the birthday of the King. The preparation for this beautiful season is not something which we shall have done for us—to be performed for us by others. This is something which we shall do ourselves—each individual and family sharing in the furnishing of this house appropriately for the celebration of Christmas—the birth of Christ.

In this spirit, we invite each of you to share in this occasion with gladness of heart in the anticipation that you, too, are making it possible for the Lord Christ to enter in. As we decorate the church and wreathe it with song, we will not only explain the history of these symbols, but we will also dedicate them and ourselves to the glory of God and his Son Jesus, our Savior.

CAROL: "O Little Town of Bethlehem"

(During the singing of this carol, the large, gold, many-pointed star is placed in position beneath the cross against the dossal hanging. At the end of the carol, the star is lighted.)

The star we place at the very center of our worship setting. The star is central in our thoughts as we recall that it was under the light of stars that the first announcement of the birth of Christ was made to the Judean shepherds.

It was the light of a star which guided the strange visitors from the East to the place where the Christ Child was. The Gospel of Matthew tells us: ". . . and lo, the star, which they saw in the east, went before them, till it came and stood over where the young child was. When they saw the star, they rejoiced with exceeding great joy."

In some lands, including Spain, Italy, and Russia, the people would wait until the first star appeared in the sky on Christmas Eve before beginning their celebrations. It is altogether fitting that the star of Bethlehem be the first of our Christmas decorations and that it occupy the central spot in our church.

CAROL (chorus only): "We Three Kings"

(Toward the end, the poinsettia plants are brought to the chancel.)

Next, we place our poinsettia plants. The gay poinsettia is rapidly becoming the most popular Christmas flower. The poinsettia is a tropical plant. Many churches are decorated with this lovely plant during this season. Contrary to general belief, the red leaves are not the blossoms; rather the small yellow flowers in the center of the cluster are the blossoms.

(Plants are tipped so that the congregation can see the blossoms.)

The poinsettia was first discovered in 1828 in Mexico by Dr. Joel R. Poinsett. The Mexicans have a legend that when blood fell on the earth from the broken heart of a young girl, a poinsettia grew from each drop. The star-shaped formation of red leaves is a reminder to us of the star which shone over Bethlehem's stable.

CAROL: "There's a Song in the Air"

(While this is sung, poinsettias are placed on stands on either side of the Communion table.)

THE GREENS

Organ: Plays "Deck the Halls," while people carrying the Christmas rope and two large wreaths for the chancel wall come to the chancel, and those with greens for the windows take their places at each window.

The greens which we use for our Christmas decorations found their way into early festivities because of certain virtues attributed to them by the ancients, and many of them which adorned pagan seasonal rites were later taken over to grace the ceremonies and celebrations of Christmas Day. The graceful custom has its roots in the profound reverence of the ancients for all natural phenomena. One thing is certain: the greens were never sought merely for their decorative capabilities, as is apt to be the case now. We should think of the garlands in a sacramental way, as carrying with them a blessing into the home and church.

The laurel and the bay symbolize victory and triumph; the yew and the cypress, eternal life. Mistletoe is regarded as a symbol of peace; and Christians came to see in the prickly leaves and the bright red berries of the holly, symbols of the crown of thorns and the sacrifice which the Christ Child, grown to manhood, made on Calvary.

God is everywhere in nature—in sky and water,

mountain and valley, grove and meadow. Let us honor and praise the God of nature.

Christmas! the joyous period of the year,
Now with bright holly all your temple strow
With laurel green and sacred mistletoe.

Green groweth the holly,
  So doth the ivy,
The God of life can never die,
Hope! saith the holly.

(Greens bearers step forward together, place greens; when all are in place, exit together.)

CAROL: "The Holly and the Ivy" or "Deck the Halls"

THE TREES

CHOIR: "O Christmas Tree, O Christmas Tree"
(While the choir is singing, the two white Christmas trees are brought to the chancel.)

Traditions concerning the Christmas tree are centuries old. An old German legend tells about Saint Winfred, a missionary to the Scandinavians in the eighth century. The people, led by their Druid priests, had gathered in the forest under a great oak to offer a human sacrifice. Saint Winfred, shocked by such brutality, and with surprising courage, hewed down the oak. As it fell, a young fir tree appeared, as if miraculously, in its place. Saint Winfred proclaimed the fir tree holy, saying it was a symbol of endless life because its leaves are ever green.

FIRST READER: These, we are told, were Winfred's words: "Take up the fir tree and carry it to the Chieftain's hall. You shall go no more into the shadows of the forest to keep your feasts with secret rites of shame. You shall keep them at home with laughter and songs and rites of love, gathered around the fir tree to rejoice in the birth night of Christ."

SECOND READER: The use of the pine and cedar is generally believed to be of German origin and ascribed to Martin Luther. Remembering his tender interest in children and the Nativity, the inspiration may well have proceeded from him. The great reformer, it is said, wandered out one Christmas Eve

and became entranced with the wonder and beauty of the starry sky. Looking up, he thought of Him "who for men and our salvation, came down from heaven." On his return home, he set up a tree for his children and decorated it with candles to represent the gracious heavens that had sent forth the little Lord Jesus.

FIRST READER: But how did the Christmas tree find its way into the church? On Christmas Eve in 1851, a young minister, Pastor Henry Schwan, newly arrived from Germany, created an uproar in the Zion Church of Cleveland, Ohio. His act was declared "sacrilegious," a "plain case of idolatry," and "groveling before shrubs." The pastor was given to understand that the town's decent citizens would not tolerate pagan practices.

SECOND READER: Pastor Schwan set out to prove that the decorated tree was not a pagan practice nor an innovation, but a thoroughly Christian custom. After long and weary research, he proved to his congregation that it was a custom known even in America. It was the young pastor who first gave the Christmas tree its traditional place beside the altar of many an American church.

WORDS BY MINISTER: We read in Isaiah, "The glory of Lebanon shall come unto thee—the fir tree, the pine tree, and the box together, to beautify the place of my sanctuary."

The psalmist said that he "whose delight is in the law of the Lord . . . shall be like a tree, planted by rivers of water." As you now place these trees in the church, let each of us, as we look upon them, turn to the God who touches earth with beauty and pray,
  "Like the straightness of the pine tree,
  Let me upright be."

(Tree bearers place trees on platform and exit together.)

CHOIR: "Gather Around the Christmas Tree"
(While the choir is singing "Gather Around the Christmas Tree," the tree bearers exit . . . and then the bearers of symbolic gift boxes take their places by each tree.)

The trees in our church are white. The white tree stands in our midst as a reminder of the completely pure and entirely unselfish love of God. It was this love which prompted him to give his only Son for our salvation. Even as the snow falls on everyone and everything, making no distinctions among any, so the white tree is a reminder of the grace of God and his unlimited love.

The white tree reminds us that giving for others, not just getting for ourselves, is the greatest lesson which Christmas can teach us. The custom of giving for family and friends is accepted as a matter of course. But the white tree speaks of something more than this. It proclaims the truth which Jesus taught, "If ye salute your brethren only, what do ye more than others? Be ye perfect as your Father which is in heaven is perfect."

This year, our Christmas offering is partially designated for our (special project).

(Gift bearers with symbolic boxes kneel before trees.)

We bring our treasures and our gifts;
And some of it is gold,
And some of it is frankincense,
And some is myrrh;
For some has come from plenty.
Some from joy,
And some from deepest sorrow of the soul.
(Unison)
But thou, O God, dost know the gift is love.
Our pledge of peace, our promise of goodwill.
Accept the gift and all the life we bring.
(Gift bearers place gifts at base of trees.)

CHOIR: "No Candle Was There and No Fire"
(Two candlelighters enter and stand at chancel. People stand at each window, with red candle in hand ready for placing.)

Light is a Christian symbol so old that it has the sanction of Jesus himself, who probably told his disciples not just once but many times, "Ye are the light of the world." Thus, every time a Christian lights a candle, he is, in effect, declaring his Christian faith and belief.

Candles were not commonly used by the first-century Christians, for the long days of the Mediterranean region stretched to embrace part of the night. It was when persecution drove the worshipers to the catacombs that they found it necessary to use lamps and candles. After Christians were allowed to worship openly, the custom of using candles in worship became well established.

At Christmas, the use of candles reflects our mood of quiet tenderness and flaming joy. The church services at Christmas are frequently held in a candlelit church where the mystery of the softly gleaming light reminds the worshiper of that strangely illuminated sky with its great star that guided the wise men that first Christmas.

Light our candles of Christmas present from the candle of Christmas past as a symbol of that Christian faith and joy which have continued for almost two thousand years. May it be a sign that our Christmas this year will be a happy and blessed one in heart and home, church and community.

THE MINISTER SAYS (to candlelighters): Now let us light the candles in the chancel and in the windows to signify that we pray for the coming of Christ into our hearts this Christmastide as never before and to testify to all men of that True Light which it is the privilege of the church to bear.
(Candlelighters move through church, lighting candles in windows.)

HYMN: "Light of the World, We Hail Thee"
"Arise, shine, for thy light is come, and the glory of the Lord is risen upon thee. The people that walked in darkness have seen a great light; they that dwell in the land of the shadow of death, upon them hath the light shined" (Isaiah 60:1; 9:2, KJV).

MINISTER AND PEOPLE: To the Prince of Peace, we now dedicate these our symbols of the Nativity, the Advent Season, and our Christian Faith. O God, we now dedicate our lives anew to the service of Christ and pray that they may be filled with thy love, so perfectly revealed through the birth and life of thy Son, Jesus Christ our Lord. Amen.

MINISTER:
I am the spirit of Joy!
Here at the Christmastide,
Where our hearts are united,
I come to abide.

Let your candles be lighted,
Your holly be hung,
Your hearth fire be merry,
Your carols be sung!

In this of all houses,
The Christ Child will bide;
Make room for his coming,
Throw the door wide!

Hang ye the greens for his welcome,
Trim gaily your tree,
Put wreaths in your windows—
Follow me! Follow me!

ALL SING SOFTLY: "Silent Night, Holy Night"
(Lights dimmed so that candlelight and light of the star dominate.)

BENEDICTION: Blessed be the God and Father of our Lord Jesus Christ, who hath blessed us with all spiritual blessings in Christ.

May the Lord of peace be with you all, this Christmas season and forever. Amen. □

ADVENT

an intergenerational celebration of Advent

EVENINGS

Cookies, candles, cards, cones, Chrismons, and crèches. These several articles were symbolic expressions of our celebration of Advent at Royersford Baptist Church.

Following successful, intergenerational church school and vacation church school experiences during the summer months in our church, I was intrigued with the possibility of trying this formula during the Advent season. After all, is there a more festive occasion in the life of the Christian community?

The Advent season is a time for families to be together. It is a time for young and old to put aside some of their suspicions and inhibitions. It is a time for the contemplation and preparation of gifts. It is a time for all within the Christian family to celebrate that joy which God has provided in life through Jesus Christ.

In sharing this idea with the board of Christian education, my "hunch" about the possibilities of this approach to the celebration of Advent was confirmed. The board's enthusiasm was apparent but tempered by several important questions: "Should we substitute this program for the meaningful peer experiences that this season provides in our church school classes? Can we design a program that will include all ages and all families? How can we effectively and helpfully handle the concern of those who prefer 'to do it the way we've always done it'? Will people participate in a program that requires some of their time in this busy Christmas season?"

These and other questions were referred to a committee selected to design and implement these "Advent Evenings," as we were to call them. This committee's proposal for a program to encompass the four Sunday evenings of Advent follows:

Purpose: To provide opportunities for persons to
- share in a meaningful way in the celebration of Christmas with their family and church
- discover or rediscover the joy in the creating and giving of gifts (including the giving of one's self)
- increase their understanding of the love and need of family members for one another.

Biblical Base: Isaiah 9:6a; 1 Corinthians 12:4-7

Devotional Theme: "Our Many Different Gifts"

Approach: On each of the first three Sunday evenings in Advent, family units (two or more persons from the same or different families) chose a "gift" to make together. These gifts were made in one of the following activity centers: making candles, designing greeting cards, baking cookies, decorating Chrismons,* constructing crèches, and creating pine-cone wreaths. A short devotional at the conclusion of each evening focused on the meaning of gifts and the different ways we might share them.

On the final Sunday evening in Advent a dessert supper was followed by a Christmas program in which several families shared. Those interested then went caroling and distributed some of the gifts created during the previous Sunday evenings. Families were encouraged to bring guests (especially those who might live alone) and to include others in their family group. Adults and youth were asked to be mindful especially of younger children and visitors and of their need to be included in the activities.

Richard Sammer is a member of the Royersford Baptist Church, Royersford, Pennsylvania.

*Note the article "Make a Chrismon Tree" on page 27.

by Richard Sammer

Proposed Schedule for First Three Sunday
    Evenings:
      6:00–6:15 Opening Activity and Directions
      6:15–7:15 "Gift Making" in Centers
      7:15–7:25 Clean Up of Centers
      7:25–7:30 Devotional Thought
      7:30–7:45 Light Refreshments
Proposed Schedule for Final Sunday Evening:
      6:00–6:45 Dessert Supper
      6:45–7:00 Carol Singing
      7:00–7:30 Family Christmas Program
      7:30–7:45 Caroling

As the overall coordinator for Advent Evenings, I asked three other persons to take specific responsibilities. One person was responsible for gathering the materials needed to make the gifts and for the recruitment and training of those individuals who would coordinate the gift making each Sunday evening. A second person was responsible for the promotion and publicity of Advent Evenings. She made colorful posters for the classrooms, prepared announcements for the newsletter and worship bulletins, and shared a story with the local newspaper. The third individual arranged for refreshments each evening and for the dessert supper on the final evening.

These persons recruited others to help them with their specific responsibilities. Attention in their recruiting was given to those persons who were not presently engaged in teaching a church school class.

One of the more important parts of our program during the first three Advent Evenings was the opening activity. Silly, get-acquainted games with a distinctive Christmas flavor were invented. Name tags helped to alleviate the embarrassment of not knowing someone's name and greatly facilitated the building of community, especially among our visitors.

A friend brought his camera and took pictures during the first two Sunday evenings. His color slides were later used in our Christmas program and were received with considerable laughter and enthusiasm. They helped us to reflect upon our experience together during these Advent Evenings and encouraged us to share some of our feelings about the making of gifts and the building of relationships.

Needless to say, we intend to repeat this experience at Royersford Baptist Church. The concern of those who prefer "to do it the way we've always done it" seemed to vanish as they were enveloped in the spirit generated. The question about the participation of "busy people in the busy Christmas season" was quickly answered when more than a hundred persons crowded into our fellowship hall each evening, several for the first time.

It is important to note that all of our program, including the gift-making centers, was staged in our fellowship hall. This "closeness" seemed appropriate and greatly aided our efforts to build community.

The above description was tailored to our particular situation, of course, and does not detail many of the activities involved. I am convinced, however, that this plan might be adapted to suit practically any situation, be it large or small, rural or urban. I would encourage you to take whatever ideas appeal to you in this description and design your own intergenerational celebration of Advent.

A definition of the word "celebrate," which amply describes our recent experience, is "to observe a notable occasion with festivities." What more "notable occasion" is there in the life of the Christian community than the birth of Christ? And what more appropriate way is there to observe this occasion than with Christian family and friends? Cookies, candles, cards, cones, Chrismons, and crèches were more than expressions of our creativity. They were symbols of our oneness in Jesus Christ—young and old, weak and strong, male and female—now and forever.   □

"Christmas Around the World"

An Evening at Church for the Entire Family

by Leonard Wilmot

It was the day after Thanksgiving, and Ruth skipped up the walk the minute she saw the mailman coming down the hill. "Have you a letter for me?" she asked. "No, but I have one for your whole family," said the mailman with a smile. Still outdoors, Ruth opened the letter and read:

Travel Reservations:
    For Your Entire Family
    To Spend Christmas with Families in
      Mexico
      India
      Japan
      Germany
      Sweden
    Education Building of the Myers Park
    Baptist Church
    Thursday evening, December 1
Tour Director:
    The Committee on Children's Work of the Board
    of Christian Education

"Mother! Mother! It's the letter about the Christmas Festival.[1] Is our whole family going?"

"Yes, Ruth, our whole family is going. We'll plan our table centerpiece tonight after Martha has gone to bed. You and I and Daddy can all work together!"

That afternoon Mother and Ruth read over the material about Christmas in the Netherlands and decided to make their centerpiece by placing Ruth's Dutch dolls standing back to back on the middle of a Styrofoam base with a wooden shoe on either

end and evergreens around the entire arrangement. In one wooden shoe they would place carrots for Saint Nicholas's horses and in the other, small gift-wrapped packages to show how the shoes would look after Saint Nicholas had called. Ruth enjoyed preparing their family's contribution. She also helped Lynn and her mother decorate some piñatas and fill them with candy for the Christmas-in-Mexico room.

However, lest we get ahead of our story, early in August when our committee on children's work was planning goals for the coming year, they decided to repeat last year's Christmas Festival. They planned once more an evening when the whole family would be together from the time they arrived at church until the time they went home. Everything would be planned to help unite families in their observance of the birthday of the Christ child. This year's theme would be "Christmas Around the World," in the hope that the evening would be a more enriching experience for school-aged boys and girls as well as their parents and other adults. They also agreed that the purpose of this year's festival would be to help every family in our congregation grow in appreciation of the contribution which people of all lands and races make to our observance of Christmas. Though the dining room would feature Christmas anywhere in the world, the committee planned to set up the other rooms of the building around five specific countries. They chose Sweden, Germany, and Mexico because of their unique and colorful Christmas customs. In addition, Japan and India, whose observance is similar to Christmas in the United States, were chosen because of their importance as American Baptist mission fields. This would help our church school teachers to be prepared more adequately to make the world outreach units of our curriculum more meaningful to their boys and girls. The committee hoped to involve as many families as possible in the planning, and over 125 families actually served on committees for the festival. That night in August, each member of

Reprinted from the November, 1961, *Baptist Leader*. Used by permission.

[1]Helpful books in planning such a festival:
Christmas Everywhere, by Elizabeth Hough Sechrist; Macrae-Smith Company, Philadelphia.
Christmas Stories 'Round the World, by Lois Johnson; Rand McNally & Co., Chicago.
Christmas Customs Around the World, by Herbert H. Wernecke, Westminster Press, Philadelphia.

the committee on children's work accepted a responsibility for a subcommittee: Hostesses and Name Tags, Table Decorations, Booklet for Use in the Home (to carry out the emphasis during the entire month of December), and for each of the five rooms emphasizing Christmas in a specific country. The committee wrote to all the major embassies in Washington, and soon booklets, maps, pictures, and music began to arrive. Early in October the committee mailed a letter to most families with children in our church school, assigning them to the various subcommittees. The committee did not ask whether a family would serve but, because of the all-church nature of the project, assumed that everyone would want to participate. Their assumption proved correct, and this saved much unnecessary phoning. Moreover, because ours is a large church, a special effort was made to place on each committee a teacher from each of the departments of our church school. In this way individuals who are closely associated in their usual church work were related to different members of the church for this particular venture. This helped to build new friendship—often a difficult achievement in a large church. This also meant that each committee would plan with every age in mind. A special effort was made to be sure that each committee had families which enjoyed music, were artistic, and liked to try out new foods. Soon everyone was reading about Christmas in other lands. Therefore, it is not surprising that with great anticipation Ruth ran up the stairs and into the education building that Thursday evening.

Ruth's entire family received their passports for the tour in the form of large name tags that had been cut from blue construction paper into the shape of globes, with north and south poles in silver glitter. "Joy to the World" was written across the bottom, and there was a white strip across the middle where Ruth wrote her name in large, second-grade writing. "My family helped make these," said Sandy, as Ruth's dad helped pin on her tag.

Entering the church dining room for a United States Christmas dinner with all the fixings except dessert, they heard the words, "It's Christmas in England," followed by the bells of one of the famous English cathedrals and a medley of English carols. These, along with other Christmas music from around the world, had been put on the church's tape recorder from a series of records of Christmas music in various countries. These carols were played as dinner music during the entire meal. Across the platform at the front of the room the flags of the United Nations were banked, while in the corner a large International Christmas Tree made the occasion more festive. This tree was covered with white lights and handmade ornaments similar to those which are used on Christmas trees in homes around the world. Later, Ruth would have the fun of making some ornaments similar to

these and taking them home to place on her family's tree.

As each family sat down to eat, they paused to offer thanks, using prayers written by boys and girls in other lands. These were taken from *Children's Prayers from Other Lands,* by Dorothy Gladys Spicer.[2] The prayers were mimeographed on stiff paper so that they stood up in front of each place and were decorated with a picture suitable to the particular nation. Each family took home several to use at home during December. A variety of napkins was secured from the Wright Studio[3] to fit in with the theme. As Ruth and her family ate, they enjoyed the centerpiece at their table, "Christmas in Finland."

After the main course, Ruth's family walked around the dining room to look at the various

centerpieces made by other families. They especially enjoyed the choirboys outside an English church and the three wise men who deliver the Christmas gifts in Spain. The wise men were made of large soft drink bottles. A large elf who delivers gifts to Danish children was made from papier-mâché and sat on a book of Hans Christian Andersen's famous children's stories.

After looking at the table centerpieces, Ruth and her family began their tour in Germany. Entering the room, they heard a sextet of junior highs, dressed in native costume, singing "Silent Night" and saw the large cedar tree covered with Christmas cookies, fruit, and toys. They tasted the delicious homemade gingerbread. Then the boys and girls made small ornaments in the shape of toys to place on their home Christmas trees. Mothers and dads either helped their children or enjoyed looking at the articles from Germany on display in the room.

[2]Order from your nearest Judson Book Store.
[3]5264 Brookville Road, Indianapolis, IN 46219.

The piece of mail Ruth received

Travel Reservations
For: Your Entire Family
To: Spread CHRISTMAS
     with Families
          in
Mexico India Japan
Germany Sweden

Passport for the tour

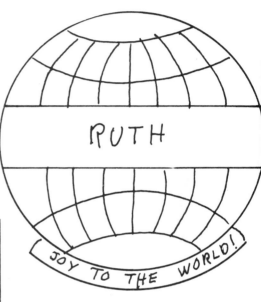

RUTH

JOY TO THE WORLD!

CHRISTMAS AROUND THE WORLD

The booklet "Christmas Around the World" which each family received to take home

Next the family entered Mexico. They were greeted at the door by a Mexican señorita, and all the adults assisting were dressed in costume. They enjoyed some cool punch served from a table decorated with poinsettias to remind us that from Mexico came our favorite Christmas flower. All around the room they saw articles from Mexico. In one corner they learned a Mexican carol as it was played on the Autoharp. The main attraction was made up of dozens of large piñatas made in the shapes of stars, animals, and birds, filled with candy, and strung across the room. One at a time boys and girls were blindfolded and tried to break the piñata. When it broke, everyone dove to the floor to get a piece of candy. "Oh, this is great fun!" said Ruth when it was her turn to hit the beautiful gold star piñata. In order to prevent confusion, only children of the same age were permitted to dive for the candy at the same time. After hitting the piñata, the family made a small one to hang on their tree at home to help them remember Christmas in Mexico. On the way out they paused at the large nativity scene and looked at the book *Nine Days of Christmas,* by Ets, from which many of the ideas in this room were taken.

By the time they arrived at India, they realized that in each land they would have some dessert which boys and girls probably enjoy at Christmas time in their country. A lady dressed in a sari served them a small paper cup of puffed wheat in brown sugar and invited them to see the Indian Christmas tree—a thorn bush decorated with Christmas cards. Other adults dressed in saris helped boys and girls make festive streamers and chains of paper bells. The family enjoyed seeing the various articles from India on display and examined the drawings which covered the entire wall of the room, which made one feel he or she had actually stepped into another land. Then the whole family stopped at the worship center where a junior teacher interpreted the nativity picture "The Visit of the Wise Men" by Bose.

The family moved on to Japan. As they arrived, a lady dressed in a kimono served them tangerines from a beautiful black laquered urn. In the background the entire wall was covered with a mural of Mount Fujiyama so that one almost seemed to have stepped into a Japanese teahouse. They sat on the floor and worked at low tables. As in all other rooms, adults familiar with the abilities of boys and girls of various ages assisted them in making ornaments for their home Christmas trees. In Japan the children make paper lanterns. Once more a beautiful arrangement of flowers on a low table beside a Japanese Madonna reminded Ruth's family that Christians the world over celebrate the birth of the Christ child by making him a member of their own people.

The smell of freshly baked cookies and wax burning greeted them as they entered the Swedish Room. At one corner a large area looked like the inside of a Swedish home. A fire burned in the fireplace, and a manikin dressed like Santa Lucia in a white gown with a wreath of candles in her hair stood beside a table ready for the Christmas Eve goodies. In another corner was a manikin dressed in a Scandinavian goat boy's uniform. Swedish Christmas dances were played on the hi-fi, delicious cookies were served, and the whole room was lighted by candles. Adults explained to the families what Swedish families do at Christmas. While mothers and dads looked further, the boys and girls made flags and paper stars—the usual Christmas tree ornaments in the Scandinavian countries.

As Ruth and her family left Sweden, they stopped to secure some UNICEF Christmas cards and received their home booklet "Christmas Around the World." In this they would find suggestions to carry the meaning of their evening at church through the entire Christmas season. For each week they would find suggestions for: "Family Worship," including bedtime prayers and grace at meals; "Family Frolic," including how they could play the piñata game as a family, make Swedish cookies, or enjoy a Christmas carol quiz; "Family Sharing," which included the addresses of missionaries in the five countries who would enjoy receiving a Christmas message; books about Christmas, or world friendship books by Friendship Press, which they might give as gifts to each other or their friends; and the recordings used in the various rooms. With their booklet and a bag full of ornaments to place on their home tree, Ruth and her family returned home after a wonderful evening of preparation for understanding the joy which comes to Christians the world over as they prepare to observe the birth of their King.

When the committee on children's work met to evaluate this occasion, they decided on one change. Next year it shall be on *two* nights so that mothers and dads who assist in the various rooms can work one night and enjoy the evening with their families the other. However, for the approximately five hundred members of our congregation who enjoyed the festival, Christmas was truly enriched by having participated, and the words of the familiar poem rang out far and clear:

> *Everywhere, everywhere, Christmas*
> *tonight!*
> *Christmas in lands of the fir tree and*
> *pine,*
> *Christmas in lands of the palm tree*
> *and vine,*
> *Christmas where snowpeaks stand*
> *solemn and white,*
> *Christmas where cornfields lie sunny*
> *and bright,*
> *Everywhere, everywhere, Christmas*
> *tonight!"*[4]

⁴By Phillips Brooks.

□

We Light Our Way to Christmas

Celebrating Advent

by Marsha West

Advent suggestions which may be used in a church worship service, in a church school worship service, or in the home.

Five fat candles, four red and one white, set into a fragrant Christmas wreath, light the way to Christmas in our church. On the fourth Sunday before Christmas the congregation enters the sanctuary to find the wreath placed on a low table in the chancel. A circle of red felt makes a simple but dramatic skirt. The candles are not lighted.

As the organ prelude comes to a close, two youngsters from the church school or Junior Choir proceed down the aisle. One of them carries a small, lighted candle. They come, very simply, to the wreath in the chancel. Five small scrolls have been tucked into the wreath at the base of the

candles. One child unrolls the scroll numbered "1" and reads the Scripture selection to the congregation. The other child then lights the first Advent candle. As the candle is lighted, the choir processional enters the sanctuary, and the congregation joins with the choir in the singing of a favorite Christmas hymn of joy. The two children quietly take their places in the congregation or with the choir. The candle is left burning throughout the service.

On each Sunday preceding Christmas an additional candle is lit, and another Bible passage heralding the coming of Christmas is read. The white candle is saved for the service on Christmas Eve.

We have found this simple ceremony an effective way to welcome Christmas together as a church. The children are impressed with the fact that they are making a valid contribution to worship. The preparation is minimal when compared with many of our elaborate and time-consuming Christmas activities. The preparation of the wreath (which of course must be treated with a good fire retardant, since it will remain in the church for some time), the selection of the Bible passages, and hymns, and a brief coaching of the children are all that is required. Here are the passages and hymns that we have found effective in our church:

First Sunday

BIBLE PASSAGE: . . . the angel Gabriel was sent from God to a city of Galilee named Nazareth, to a virgin betrothed to a man whose name was Joseph, of the house of David; and the virgin's name was Mary. And he came to her and said, "Hail, O favored one, the Lord is with you!" But she was greatly troubled at the saying, and considered in her mind what sort of greeting this might be. And the angel said to her, "Do not be afraid, Mary, for you have found favor with God. And behold, you will conceive in your womb and bear a son, and you shall call his name Jesus.

He will be great, and will be called the Son of the
   Most High;
and the Lord God will give to him the throne of his
   father David,
and he will reign over the house of Jacob for ever;
and of his kingdom there will be no end."

                  —Luke 1:26-33

HYMN: "Angels We Have Heard on High"

Second Sunday

BIBLE PASSAGE: The people who walked in
   darkness have seen a great light;
those who dwelt in a land of deep darkness
   on them has light shined.
For to us a child is born,
   to us a son is given;
and the government will be upon his shoulder,
   and his name will be called
"Wonderful Counselor, Mighty God,
   Everlasting Father, Prince of Peace."
Of the increase of his government and of peace
   there will be no end,
upon the throne of David, and over his kingdom,
   to establish it, and to uphold it
with justice and with righteousness
   from this time forth and for evermore.
The zeal of the Lord of hosts will do this.

                  —Isaiah 9:2, 6-7

HYMN: "O Come, O Come, Emmanuel"

Third Sunday

BIBLE PASSAGE: The wilderness and the dry land
   shall be glad,
the desert shall rejoice and blossom;
like the crocus it shall blossom abundantly,
   and rejoice with joy and singing.
Then the eyes of the blind shall be opened,
   and the ears of the deaf unstopped;
then shall the lame man leap like a hart,
   and the tongue of the dumb sing for joy.
For waters shall break forth in the wilderness,
   and streams in the desert;
the burning sand shall become a pool,
   and the thirsty ground springs of water. . . .

                —Isaiah 35:1-2*a*, 5-7

HYMN: "Joy to the World"

Reprinted from the November, 1968, *Baptist Leader.* Used by permission.

Fourth Sunday

BIBLE PASSAGE: There shall come forth a shoot
   from the stump of Jesse,
   and a branch shall grow out of his roots.
And the Spirit of the Lord shall rest upon him,
   the spirit of wisdom and understanding,
   the spirit of counsel and might,
   the spirit of knowledge and the fear of the Lord.
And his delight shall be in the fear of the Lord.

                          ●

. . . the mountain of the house of the Lord
shall be established as the highest of the mountains,
   and shall be raised above the hills;
and all the nations shall flow to it,
   and many peoples shall come, and say:
"Come, let us go up to the mountain of the Lord,
   to the house of the God of Jacob;
that he may teach us his ways
   and that we may walk in his paths."
For out of Zion shall go forth the law,
   and the word of the Lord from Jerusalem.
He shall judge between the nations,
   and shall decide for many peoples;
and they shall beat their swords into plowshares,
   and their spears into pruning hooks;
nation shall not lift up sword against nation,
   neither shall they learn war any more.

                          ●

They shall not hurt or destroy
   in all my holy mountain;
for the earth shall be full of the knowledge of the
   Lord
   as the waters cover the sea.

         —Isaiah 11:1-3; 2:2-4; 11:9

HYMN: "Angels, from the Realms of Glory"

Christmas Eve (or Christmas Day Service) [1]

BIBLE PASSAGE: In that region there were shepherds out in the field, keeping watch over their flock by night. And an angel of the Lord appeared to them, and the glory of the Lord shone around them, and they were filled with fear. And the angel said to them, "Be not afraid; for behold, I bring you good news of a great joy which will come to all the people; for to you is born this day in the city of David a Savior, who is Christ the Lord. And this will be a sign for you: you will find a babe wrapped in swaddling cloths and lying in a manger." And suddenly there was with the angel a multitude of the heavenly host praising God and saying,

"Glory to God in the highest,
   and on earth peace among men with whom he is
   pleased!"

                  —Luke 2:8-14

HYMN: "Hark! The Herald Angels Sing"

[1]In churches where a Christmas Eve or Christmas Day service is not held, the white candle may be omitted or may be lighted the fourth Sunday, along with reading this Bible passage.

ADVENT

ADVENTures in learning about, experiencing, and preparing for the Good News message of Christmas during the four-week period of festivities and activities that take place before December 25

by John Murrow

Have you ever asked a group of youth to list the words and phrases they think of in association with Christmas? It's interesting to hear all of the responses. Tinsel, jingle bells, gifts, wrapping presents, Santa Claus, stars, trees, bright-colored lights, carols and music, food, family, shepherds, snow, Jesus Christ, Bethlehem, pageants, candlelight, manger, the wise men—these are just some of the words that come to mind when we think of Christmas.

The weeks before December 25 are full and hectic, finding most of us frantically buying gifts, spending money that we don't have, or getting caught up and crushed in mobs of people. Amidst the confusion is also an excitement that is very special to that time of the year. But by the time Christmas Day arrives, many of us are on the verge of exhaustion. This is not to say that all the efforts were in vain, that energies and time were wasted, or that the motives for all of the running around were insincere. Christmas should be an extraordinary occasion, and festive times that remain in our memories require much time and preparation.

For Christians Christmas is a most significant occasion. Each of us could use the weeks before Christmas more wisely, directing our actions and thoughts to what Christmas is really all about. We can spend our time and energies in ways that enable us to grow in the Christian faith, experience the presence of God through Christ in our own lives, relate this to one another, and share with others.

For some people the word "advent" itself is unfamiliar. It comes from a Latin word meaning "to arrive, to come forward." Thus, it means it is a time of getting ready for the festival season, the celebration of Christmas and the coming of Jesus Christ, the Messiah. During this time our thoughts and actions should be focused on the joyful event of Christ's birth. Advent is a time of expectation, of anticipating three specific events: (1) the birth of Jesus Christ, (2) the hope of his return, and (3) his continued presence in the lives of those who are prepared for and willing to receive him. We ought to consider some of the activities that we do before Christmas, asking ourselves why we participate in them and what the meaning behind them is. If we do, we might come to realize that some of them don't have much to do with the true message of Christmas. Some of them we will discard and no longer use. But in the process we might also discover new activities which enhance the Christmas message, making it clearer in our own lives and showing others what it means. The following suggestions are to help you do just that. They are resources to stimulate your thinking about the ways we celebrate Christmas. Use them with your own youth group just as they appear, or implement them in other ways. Incorporate some of them with activities that youth in your church are already doing and finding meaningful. Combine or adapt the activities to

The author is the Associate Minister of Mountview Baptist Church, Columbus, Ohio.

fit your own needs. Create your own ideas and try them. You'll find that not all of the suggestions will work for you. Some you may use only once, while others can become traditions that you expand and develop from year to year. Don't try to use all of them at once—or even in the same year. Select a few that seem to interest most of the youth and try those. Keep in mind that these are intended to help both individuals and the entire group to prepare spiritually for Christmas.

A Announce.

Christmas is God's announcement to us, his people. The reason that we have for celebrating the birth of Jesus Christ is recorded in the Old and New Testament Scriptures. God announces to us in the Bible the coming of Jesus Christ into our own lives, his presence with us. To provide depth and purpose to the events and activities in which we participate, it is important to read and study in order to know what God is telling us. Some references to begin with include: Genesis 1:1-15; Isaiah 9:2-7; 52:7-10; 62:10-12; Matthew 1:18—2:23; Luke 2:1-20; John 1:1-18; and Colossians 1:15-20. You'll have other passages that might be helpful, too. Along with study and reading, find music that describes what you are learning; or write your own songs, poems, or prayers that express what God is announcing to us.

D Decorate.

Visual symbols of the season are important for us in depicting the Christmas message. In addition to the study of specific Bible passages, it's helpful to visualize the announcement through the use of symbols. Decorations for Christmas have taken on many forms. Christians can do better in showing the truth of Christmas than using store-bought plastic reindeer and Santa Claus statues or even tin soldiers. Ornaments can be created that symbolically and genuinely express Christian faith. Some may want to make a large banner out of scraps of felt and burlap. Hang it in a prominent place where everyone will enjoy

it. An advent wreath may be made, the circle showing the endless nature of God's love for us through Christ, and the four candles standing for the four weeks of Advent. A candle in the center represents Christ. Create your own ceremony, and light a candle each week. Some may want to make mobiles out of wire, displaying them in your church lobby or classrooms. If your church already has a tree, you might like to make some Chrismons (monograms symbolic of the Christian faith). These can be easily made by cutting forms (such as stars, crosses, fish) out of Styrofoam. Plan a time to involve not only members of your youth group but their families as well. After the fun of making the ornaments, join together in decorating your church family tree and sing familiar carols. A large pine-cone wreath might interest some. Use acorns and other natural objects from God's creation to make it. Decorations are another way of showing the Good News message.

V "Venite Adoremus."

O Come, Let Us Adore Him. Let's find ways to express and worship the birth of Christ. Your group might have special ability to work on a skit that is already written—or even an original. Special pageants could be planned. Some members of your group might have musical or poetic talent. Discuss with your pastor and others who are responsible for times of worship how you might participate in sharing and preparing for the coming of Christmas. You might design a contemporary form of worship, using various Bible passages, incorporating candlelight, drama, and music that speaks to you. You might include some of the art forms or other decorations that you've been creating as a time of celebration together in the name of the Lord.

E Excitement.

As Christmas gets closer, the momentum seems to increase. Plan times when you can get together as a group, such as a progressive supper. Some groups might want to have a "lock-in," a retreat—at the church—which has been planned by youth and advisers where you can stay in the building and make decorations, sing, tell stories, have Bible study, show movies, and conclude with a simple breakfast. Some groups might take orders for cookies and other baked goods prior to the lock-in, cook during that night, and deliver the articles the next morning. You might want to have the group in front of a large fireplace, if you're fortunate enough to have one, either at the church, or in the home of one of your members or friends. This provides a great setting to discuss such things as what Christmas means to you. You might ask everyone to bring a picture, magazine article, poem, or something which begins discussion as to what Christmas is. You might share customs and traditions that you have within your own family, how Christmas is celebrated throughout the world, customs, foods, and so on. It's also a good idea to talk about those practices of Christmas that we'd like to continue and those which might detract from our celebration.

Nativity.

Christmas is the birth of Jesus the Christ. We can explore ways that we can experience what actually happened around that event in Bethlehem. You might already have some type of Christmas pageant. Some groups create a living manger scene, with real people, straw, and animals. Depending on your local situation, you can adapt or adopt this idea. You might have a large parking lot or area around your church where people could drive by and see this. Or, you could have various stopping points—inside or outside—where people would also see slides from the areas in which Jesus lived and taught, hear special Christmas carols, and finish their little trek with refreshments. Other groups might think about making papier-mâché or wooden figures, which could be used in a pageant with younger children. Another idea is to make a silhouette and light it on the outside or inside of your church. This could take the form of a manger, a star, or some other design that would relate that the message of Christmas is "God with us."

Tell Everyone!

The meaning of the Good News of God's love at Christmas cannot be kept to ourselves—it has to be shared with other people. To those who are sick, lonely, poor, without family, imprisoned, or in other circumstances where life seems meaningless and hopeless, Christmas can be a sad time. We can share the love of God through Christ with others. You might invite people to a supper that you have planned or to the decoration party. You might give decorations to those who are shut-in, and tell them what the symbols mean. Caroling, making fruit or food baskets, and collecting food for neighborhood food pantries are important ways you can share God's love. Some projects that have begun during the Advent season ought to be continued throughout the year. In place of exchanging gifts with one another in your own group, it would be great to obtain the names of other youth and find out if they have "wish lists," items that they want for Christmas that you can sign up to purchase individually or as a group. Such requests can be obtained through your city, county, or state department of children's services. There are so many ways that your efforts and energies can be directed to other people. Our lives can reflect, through our time and sharing, the true spirit of Christmas—namely, enthusiastically giving of ourselves and sharing what we have, as Christ taught us.

Remember, whatever your group decides to do in preparation for Christmas, begin with the purpose and depth of the message as told to us in the Bible. From that point, there are countless ways that you can focus on the birth of Jesus and his message. Plan several activities that seem to interest most of the members of your group. It's better to do a few things well than to become frustrated in trying too much and not accomplishing anything. It is hoped that you will have a better understanding and deeper appreciation of why we as Christians celebrate this great holiday. Enjoy it, have fun, and grow together! □

An Advent Worship Suggestion for Youth

● by Franklin Nelson

Advent is traditionally the "Christmas season." For the church it is a season of preparation during the four weeks before December 25. An Advent worship celebrates the ADVENTure of Christ in our past, present, and future.

HE HAS COME;

HE IS COMING DAILY;

and HE WILL NEVER STOP COMING,

BUT WILL COME AGAIN.

PEACE LOVE JOY HOPE

CELEBRATE HIS COMING!

Have an Advent worship as part of a Christmas workshop.

Use it with a gathering of youth in the community.

Worship in the Advent season is a preparation for his coming into our lives. It is hoped that a worship service is never a show or a performance but, rather, something that we do that celebrates the relationship we have with God through Jesus Christ.

The following is a design for an Advent worship service which celebrates the coming of *hope, joy, peace,* and *love.* You make it your own service when God's Spirit moves through it to you and it becomes an experience of worship. Use it in a creative way with all the changes and variations that are necessary for your unique situation.

The author is the Associate Pastor of First Baptist Church, Davenport, Iowa.

Lead in your church's morning or evening worship service.

Gather the members of your church's youth together for an Advent service.

HELPS BEFORE YOU BEGIN

Option one: For each of the themes in the worship you may want to light a candle.

Option two: Or you may want to bring in banners of Hope, Joy, Peace, Love.

Option three: Or you might want to unscramble play

blocks with letters on them. For example:

E	O	H	P	would become	H

					O
					P
					E

Y	O	J	would become	J

| | | | | O |
| | | | | Y |

If you can't find enough blocks, make your own from a 2' x 4' board and some bright paints.

CALL TO WORSHIP (Bringing the outside in.)

Prepare beforehand a cassette recording of some outside sounds, such as:

School bell ringing
Car honking in heavy traffic
Children playing
Cash register
Sound of a time clock being punched
(You think of some more.)

And then add at the end:

A scream! and
The crying of a baby. (The crying will, for us, be the birth of Christ into this worship service.)

INVOCATION

Leader: Let us all pray!

Lord God, you have filled our past. You are filling our present moment, and you will fill our future together with hope and joy,
peace and love.
Thank you for the crying of a baby long ago that brought hope to our own futures, joy to our spirits, peace to our minds, and love to our relationships. Thank you for the coming of Jesus Christ into our lives.

Amen.

Song: Choose a song your group knows well, such as "He's Everything to Me" or "The First Noel" or one that fits for you.

Speaker of Hope: Because Jesus Christ has come and is coming, we live in HOPE. *(The Speaker of Hope acts as the leader for the HOPE section.)*
People: We live in HOPE.
(Speaker lights a candle, unscrambles the H-O-P-E blocks, or both.)
Scripture Reading: Isaiah 9:2
Experience of Darkness: If your group is small enough, provide blindfolds for all the people. If it is a large group, have all close their eyes. Suggest that they are in total darkness. They are blind. "You are beginning to feel despair and panic, and there is no hope!" The Speaker of Hope reads the following poem or one that you might write about darkness and despair:

I ran down city streets
to an alley of despair
And down steps of failure
to the tunnel of darkness
And there learned
fear and coldness,
smell of dankness,
hopelessness.
A tunnel to take you
to the other side
but only leaves you
beaten at the end
of a tunnel
that has no end.

SILENT MEDITATION

Speaker: This is the message of despair, but out of despair is born hope. Lift your blindfolds (or eyelids) and see the light within 1 John 1:5-7. *(Then read the Scripture.)*
Because Jesus Christ has come and is coming, we live in HOPE.
People: We live in HOPE.
Speaker: Let us sing verse three of "Hark! the Herald Angels Sing."

Speaker of Joy: Because Jesus Christ has come and is coming, we live in JOY.

People: We live in JOY.

> *(Speaker lights the second candle or unscrambles the J-O-Y blocks, or both.)*

Scripture Reading: Isaiah 9:3

LITANY

Prophet of God: We are the new Israel. The people of God.

People of God: How do you know?

Prophet of God: By the promises of the God who created us and who has spoken to us his Word.

People of God: We're a "second chance" people. We flopped and messed up, but God brought us back and accepted us.

Prophet of God: He did this when Jesus, our King, was born in Bethlehem.

People of God: There is pain in birth.

Prophet of God: There is pain in JOY.

EXPRESSIONS OF JOY

Call on one to three persons of your group to share expressions of joy. Be sure to ask them ahead of time to take no more than one to two minutes.

Speaker: Because Christ came and is coming, we live in JOY.

People: We live in JOY.

Speaker: Let us sing verse one of "Joy to the World."

Speaker of Peace: Because Jesus Christ has come and is coming, we live in PEACE.

People: We live in PEACE. *(Speaker lights a candle or unscrambles the P-E-A-C-E blocks, or both.)*

The Reading of Some Bad News: Have two to four persons read from the newspaper brief excerpts that describe unrest or war between nations or within families. Be sure to ask the readers ahead of time. (You might want to use Simon and Garfunkel's recording of "Silent Night," found on their *Parsley Sage* album, as a background for the newspaper reading.)

The Reading of Some Good News: Isaiah 9:6-7

Speaker: Blessed are the peacemakers, for they shall be called the sons of God. Because Jesus Christ has come and is coming, we live in PEACE.

People: We live in PEACE.

Speaker: Let us sing verse one of "Hark! the Herald Angels Sing"

Speaker of Love: Because Jesus Christ came and is coming, we live in LOVE.

People: We live in LOVE.

> *(Speaker lights a candle or unscrambles the L-O-V-E blocks, or both.)*

Scripture Reading: 1 John 2:9-11

EXPRESSIONS OF LOVE

Ask someone beforehand to prepare a brief sermon, three to five minutes long. Use the above Scripture and the theme "Christmas Means Love."

Scripture Reading: 1 John 4:9-10

Speaker: Because Jesus Christ came and is coming, we live in LOVE.

People: We live in LOVE.

Speaker: Let us stand to sing the last verse of "Joy to the World." *(Remain standing)*

(From where they are seated, all four speakers join in the litany.)

LITANY

Speaker of Hope: Because Jesus Christ has come and is coming, we live in HOPE.

People: We live in HOPE.

Speaker of Joy: Because Jesus Christ has come and is coming, we live in JOY.

People: We live in JOY.

Speaker of Peace: Because Jesus Christ has come and is coming, we live in PEACE.

People: We live in PEACE.

Speaker of Love: Because Jesus Christ has come and is coming, we live in LOVE.

People: We live in LOVE.

All: And we live together in today's world as people of Christ.

THE SENDING FORTH

Record a second cassette using the same sounds as in the CALL TO WORSHIP, but put the sound of the scream and the infant baby crying first.

Scripture Reading (One of the speakers should read this during the recording after the baby's crying stops.): Luke 4:18-21.

At the end of the sounds, or the Scripture, the Leader will say simply:

> "We are sent forth in today's world as people of HOPE, as people of JOY, as people of PEACE, as people of LOVE, as people of GOD." □
>
> Amen.

MAKE A "CHRISMON" TREE

For Fun, Fellowship, and Meaning

• by Nancy Stringer

Some of the Chrismons we made

We made Chrismons last Christmas! And what are they? Chrismons are Christmas decorations made in the shapes of Christian symbols. Hung on an evergreen tree, they make a "Chrismon" tree.

We first learned about Chrismons when our Advent committee for 1976 was considering ideas for an Advent evening workshop. We wanted something in which persons of all ages could participate. We wanted something that would be fun to do together and also would be meaningful. Our senior minister, the Reverend Dale Lock, pastor of the First Baptist Church of Pittsfield, Massachusetts, suggested making Chrismons for a Chrismon tree. He showed us some pictures, and we became very enthusiastic.

Mr. Lock gave us two books: *Chrismons, Basic Series,* published by the Lutheran Church of the Ascension of Danville, Virginia, where the Chrismon tree originated in 1957; and *Chrismons* by Francis Kipps Spencer, a member of the Lutheran Church of the Ascension, who designed the first Chrismons.

From these books we learned that the word "Chrismon" is a combination of parts of two words— *CHRISt* and *MONogram.* Monograms of Christ are symbols that honor the name of our Lord Jesus Christ. Chrismon symbols proclaim the events of the life and saving acts of Christ. Many of these symbols were used by the first Christians to identify themselves to one another and to designate places to meet and worship, often in secret. Even more important was the use of these symbols of Christ by the early Christians to share and pass on their faith. Making Chrismons together would be a good way to learn about the history and meanings of symbols, and making Chrismons would help us to share and pass on our faith.

In our reading, we learned that Chrismons are made in color combinations of white, gold, and silver to symbolize the purity and majesty of the Son of God. The evergreen tree, which symbolizes the eternal life

Mrs. Stringer is Superintendent of the Primary Department of the First Baptist Church, Pittsfield, Massachusetts.

Making Chrismons

which our Savior gave us, is a background for the Chrismons. Tiny white lights are strung on the tree to represent the Light of the world. What beautiful symbolisms! This special tree, we felt, would surely put Christ at the center of our Christmas celebration!

We started immediately to plan a Chrismon workshop. Mr. Lock had already obtained copyright permission for our church to use the Chrismon idea. Permission can be obtained very easily by sending a request to the Lutheran Church of the Ascension, 295 W. Main Street, Danville, VA 24541. The only limitation is that Chrismons may not be made for sale. Books, such as the ones we used, with patterns, directions, and explanations of the meanings of the Chrismon symbols can also be obtained from them for a small charge.

Using the book *Chrismons, Basic Series* as a guide, our committee picked out some designs and started gathering materials for our evening workshop. Some of the materials we purchased (or were given) were sheets of white Styrofoam and white felt. These were cut into a number of basic shapes. To decorate the shapes, we gathered gold and silver spray, gold and

silver braid and sequins, gold and silver glitter, gold tinsel garland, white glue, and small pins. We also collected used Christmas cards, decoupage glaze, Styrofoam balls and cubes, glass beads, thick white pipe cleaners, and, last but not least, paper clips to use as hangers.

The committee decided that if the workshop were to be a "one-evening" event, some advance preparation needed to be done. We recruited a few more committee members and went to work one morning a week in one another's homes, cutting out all the Styrofoam shapes needed and spraying them with gold and silver paint. Cutting the Styrofoam seemed to be a problem at first. It is soft and easily breakable—cutting it with scissors didn't work at all. We got good results, however, cutting it with a straightedged knife. But the best method is to use a knife with a serrate edge and to saw slowly along a pencil line. Our work went fast after we discovered this. Our children, who accompanied us at the work sessions, kept busy and happy picking up the scraps of Styrofoam, as we cut, and decorating them with their crayons. We laughed about the tiny Styrofoam bits that stuck to everything, even us!

The completed Chrismon tree

Decorating the Chrismon tree

The EPIPHANY STAR is symbolic of the Manifestation to the wise men.

"...and lo, the star which they had seen in the East went before them, till it came to rest over the place where the child was." Matthew 2:9b

The ROSE is symbolic of Mary the mother of Jesus, or of His human birth.

All references in this series were taken from <u>Chrismons</u> by Frances Kipps Spencer.

This appeared in the "Visitor"— the church's newsletter.

THE CHRISMON WORKSHOP is Sunday evening, December 5th. The Senior Highs will serve a light supper at 6:00 PM, and the workshop will begin at 7:00. Everyone can make Chrismons, adults and children too! Some Chrismons are very easy to make, some are intermediate and some are challenging. Come and help us decorate our church tree and have some Chrismons to take home too.

Reservations for the supper should be called in to the church office by Friday, December 3rd, or sign up on list posted.   Cost - 75¢ each.

Incidentally, these Styrofoam bits can be cleaned up very easily with the hose attachment of a vacuum cleaner.

We used six basic designs and made samples of each for the workshop. We recommend that a group making Chrismons for the first time use simple designs and not try to make too many different kinds. We made a star, decorated with sequins and glitter; a Greek cross, covered with even rows of silver sequins; and a fish with a metallic braid cross on it and a metallic braid around its edge to outline the shape of the fish. The committee cut tiny manger scenes from the used Christmas cards and glazed them. On the night of the workshop, people put the manger scenes into Styrofoam balls which had been cut in half and scooped out to make little "shells." The outside of the "shells" were decorated with sequins or glitter. This Chrismon was very popular with the younger children.

A "sun of righteousness" Chrismon was designed with a gold tinsel garland around a white felt disk, representing the sun. The disk was centered with the *PX* monogram. *P* and *X* are the first two letters of the Greek word for Christ, or Messiah. Malachi 4:2 was used with this one to explain its meaning.

A Latin cross (the one familiar to most of us) centered in a circle (to represent eternity) was made from sparkling glass beads strung on thick white pipe cleaners.

We made some of the Chrismon materials into "plastic sandwich bag" kits, in which we included all the necessary materials for a Chrismon. Other decorating materials we left uncut so that people at the workshop could made their own original designs.

In planning the workshop, one concern was to have some Chrismons easy enough for young children to make, some that would be challenging enough for the artistically talented, and some for everyone in between. In making the designs ourselves, we found some to be much easier than others. This helped us to label each design "very easy," "intermediate," or "challenging." We told the congregation in advance that there would be these three grades, in order to reassure those who might think they're not "creative" enough to participate in such a workshop.

To spark the interest of our congregation, we ran a series of articles on Chrismons in our weekly newsletter, "First Baptist Visitor." The first article explained the meaning of the Chrismon tree and where it originated; it told about the Chrismon workshop that was being planned. Each week, for the next five weeks, one or two different Christian symbols were featured, with drawings and an explanation of their meanings. The sixth and final article included an invitation to everyone to come to the workshop.

Excitement mounted among the committee members as we saw our progress from week to week in preparing for the workshop. It was fun designing the different Chrismons and seeing our finished samples. Ideas for decorating them seemed to come to us faster than we could work them out. And as we worked, we got to know one another better! We looked forward to our Tuesday morning work session and couldn't wait to share our preparations with our whole congregation. Our one disappointment came when our state legislature passed a law banning the use of natural trees in public places, including churches, because of the assumed fire hazard. We were nearly finished with our Chrismon preparations at that point. Fortunately, one of our members donated a six-foot green artificial tree for our use.

Finally, the night of the workshop arrived. After one of our delicious church suppers served by the senior highs, we brought out the boxes of prepared materials and spread them on the tables with the finished samples and signs, labeling them "very easy," "intermediate," or "challenging." Then everyone started to work. Some copied the samples. Others created their own original designs. Even young children made Chrismons with the help of a mother, father, older brother, or sister. Everyone had a great time!

We suggested that people make one Chrismon for the church tree and one to take home. At the end of the one-and-one-half-hour workshop, the tree was ladened with Chrismons; people were still working enthusiastically; and almost all the materials were used. Those of us who had been on the committee were happy that everyone had such a good time!

Looking back, a short service, with caroling around the tree, would have been an appropriate way to end the evening. As it was, we had no formal ending.

Still, the evening was a success. The tree was beautiful, its meaning very special; and it was uniquely ours because we had made it. And we have started something that can be a joy to us for many years to come as we design and add new Chrismons to the ones we already have.   □

A Children's Christmas Eve Service

• **by J. Russell Raker, Jr.**

Each year I am faced with the question: Do you have an 11 P.M. candlelight Christmas Eve service; do you have one earlier—7 or 7:30 P.M.? If both are held, then the 100 to 125 people are divided into two smaller groups, and most of the folks like the late service. Last year I tried something else—a 7 P.M. service for "children only" from four years through fourth grade.

I listed the potential by ages and grades. I sent a letter to the parents listing the children's names, giving them an idea of the program, and enclosing a card for their return. This was sent out on December 1. In the letter I suggested that their children might have friends whose names I didn't have, and if they would like to have them invited, the parents could phone and give me the names. I received several who were not going to

The Reverend J. Russell Raker, Jr., is Pastor of the First Baptist Church of Chittenango, New York.

any church school and who became prospects for our school.

As soon as the cards came back, I sent a second letter thanking the parents and saying how pleased I was that their children were coming to the service. I told them, again, that the service would be exactly one hour long. If they had sent the names of additional children, I thanked them and suggested that they might bring those children with their own. In this second letter I also announced that an offering would be taken for the children in Haiti, stating that ten cents would buy a hot meal for one child. I also sent a copy of a combination letter (combination of the two previous letters) to the parents of the children whose names were referred to me.

The cards came back very soon. I phoned those who did not answer by December 18. Several more were added to our list. I found that two who were in the fifth grade and who did not come to the 11 P.M. service wanted to come. They were allowed. There also was a family who wanted to be together for Christmas Eve but who would not be at the 11 P.M. service; nor would the parents let their daughter come to the 7 P.M. service by herself. I let them all come and asked the parents to help me.

The helpers were my wife, the above-mentioned couple, a nurse who always works Christmas Eve, and a young girl who played for the service. I began the service sitting on the edge of the platform where I had erected a cardboard fireplace, and repeated the first line or two of "'Twas the Night Before Christmas." I led from this right into the service. We sang carols that the children knew; one third grade girl read the Scripture which we had as an insert (an American Bible Society piece); and then we made a banner of the three wise men which was used in the 11 P.M. service.

The pieces had been pre-cut. Children glued them on the felt, each one taking a turn while I told them a story about the wise men. The older ones sewed a few things on the banner. This took about fifteen minutes. We ended the service with a Christmas filmstrip and a carol.

One caution. I fortunately was prepared for what might happen in the making of the banner. The children were quite young and needed a lot of guidance in putting the banner together. We had everything prepared, and I went over with the adults beforehand how the banner should look when finished. We prepared beforehand many of the time-consuming little things. If we had not done this, two things would have resulted: (1) we would not have had enough time (only fifteen minutes were allotted), and (2) we would have lost the attention of the younger ones. Because of our preparation, neither of these things happened.

We did have an offering about which the parents had been notified. (It went to one of our schools in Haiti to supply hot lunches at ten cents each.) We received over fifteen dollars from this offering.

Each child at the service—and there were thirty-six—received a small candy cane and a tree ornament that looked like stained glass and was purchased from the Judson Book Store. It was a most enjoyable evening, and, to my pleasure, the 11 P.M. service of 135 was the largest ever. I believe one helped the other.

Suggested Calendar for the Leader

December 1—prepare list of names, letter #1, and return card; mail letter and card. In letter, list names of children in the family who could come. Go over complete details with church secretary.

December 10—check acceptances against list (this is really done on a daily basis). Send out second letter. Send a combination letter to any new names received.

December 18—final date (?) for sending second letter or receiving new names.

December 20—secure bulletins for service and mimeograph them. Make sure you have enough candy canes and anything else you are going to give to the children. Select the two children you wish to hand out bulletins as the rest of the worshipers come in for the service.

On the Sunday before Christmas immediately after the morning service, meet with the adults who are going to help you so that each one knows what he or she is to do to assist. To hold the attention of these children on Christmas Eve means that every moment must be under control.

December 26 (or the first day back to the office after Christmas)—send a thank-you letter to each adult who assisted and to the parents who brought or sent their children. Thank-yous never hurt. □

CHRISTMAS AROUND THE WORLD

An Original Pageant for the Church School

● **by Barbara Bishop**

I. Processional by choirs and participants

II. Presentation of program

   A. England

Narrator 1: England, a nation steeped in pagan traditions and folklore, has contributed to the Christmas tradition in notable music and family programs. The pagan Druids originated the Yule log tradition by choosing oaken logs for sacrifice to Thor, their mightiest god. It was believed that the light and heat would drive away evil spirits, and painstaking care was taken to honor the tradition.

Pantomime the scene—background music of "Deck the Halls." The enactment should go according to the balance of the narration.

Barbara Bishop is the Church School Director of the First Baptist Church of Penn Yan, New York.

Narrator 1 (cont.): Before the log is fired, the family rises to kneel by the hearth, kiss the log, and Mother and children form a circle around the log, while Father lights it. Once the log is lit, the family joins in chorus:

Family: "Welcome be thou, heavenly king,
      Welcome, born on this morning.
      Welcome, for whom we shall sing,
      Welcome, Yule."

Narrator 2: Music is a great part of England's Christmas. One of the most popular carols is "Angels from the Realms of Glory." James Montgomery, a Moravian composer and liberal reformist, edited a journal, *The Sheffield Iris,* and for his efforts frequently sat behind prison walls. Henry Smart, the blind composer, adapted the music of this carol from old French lyrics. Let us listen to the choir and organ perform "Angels from the Realms of Glory."

Narrator 3: [*This narrator will give the background of the Boar's Head Poem, which can be found in the bibliography at the end of this article. The poem can be sung, if music is available, or recited.*]

Organ interlude: One verse of appropriate national music is used throughout to allow for clearing of stage and introduction of each country. Narrators 4, 5, and 6 move to seats nearer the podium during interludes.

B. Germany

Narrator 4: December sixth, Saint Nicholas Day, is the beginning of Advent in Germany. Nicholas, born of missionary parents in the fourth century in Asia Minor, became a bishop by chance. According to literature and tradition, it is reported that the church was futilely seeking a bishop and resolved that the first male to appear for worship would be named bishop. Nicholas, then a youth, appeared as the first worshiper on the following Sunday and was selected. During his lifetime, miracles were credited to him, and he was canonized as the patron saint of children.

Stage is now prepared for the Advent wreath and Christmas tree. Organ interlude is played.

Narrator 5: One of the loveliest German traditions is the Advent wreath. Created from simple firs, red ribbons, and candles, every home enjoys this table centerpiece.

Pantomime the scene: a family makes a wreath on stage.

Narrator 5 (cont.): Once the wreath is made, the candles are lit, four candles symbolizing the four Sundays of Advent.

Narrator 6: Originating in mythology, the Christmas tree tradition is well known around the world. Martin Luther is credited with the first decorated and lighted tree; and on the Holy Night trees are found everywhere, even in cemeteries.

Narrator 7: [*Explain the Boxer Day tradition, which can be found in the bibliography. Have a family enact the narration.*]

Stage preparation after narration—stool, mike, and spotlight. Organ interlude is played during stage preparation.

C. Austria

Narrator 8: It is 1818, a few days before Christmas in Oberdorf, Austria. Franz Gruber, organist, reports to Father Joseph Mohr that there will be no organ music on Christmas, as mice have chewed holes in the bellows, and they no longer supply air to the organ pipes. Pressured by time,

the men determine that Father Mohr will write the words and Franz Gruber the music for an all-new carol. Christ's birth is again retold in "Silent Night, Holy Night."

Carol is then played by soloist and can be sung by a vocalist. Narrator 8 can speak about community singing. The congregation can then sing two Austrian carols.

D. Italy

Narrator 9: From the heaven-reaching peaks of the Alps to the world-famous "seven hills of Rome" all eyes of Latin Christendom turn to the "Eternal City" whose Basilica of Saint Peter hosts services heralding the birth of Christ. A massive and brilliant procession of bishops, cardinals, and priests provides for the entrance of His Holiness, the pope, borne aloft on a red and gold chair. Clothed in ermine robes, encrusted in jewels, the pope passes through the nave, his fingers raised in the sign of the Trinity, blessing the worshipers who jam the basilica.

Narrator 10: [*Can speak of the great spiritual meaning of Christmas in "O Holy Night."*]

Narrator 11: Small villages along the foothills of the Alps and Apennines have little contact with the magnificence at Vatican City; so traditions of uniqueness have developed over the years. A few days before Christmas, bagpipers move through the villages, playing carols, leaving wooden spoons as symbols of blessings for a bountiful harvest. Families provide foodstuffs and money to the players.

Families 1 and 2 are used to enact this narration.

Narrator 11 (cont.): The Italian child is raised to honor his/her parents, and on Christmas Day comes a touching, loving letter from child to parent.

Scene: Through a microphone, a child "writes" but actually reads a prepared letter to his parents. Stage is cleared and set up with table in center. Spotlight is used.

E. France

Narrator 12: [*Speaks of Saint Barbara's Day (check the bibliography for information). Narrator 12 also leads kindergarten children into the creation of the crèche.*]

The French tradition is, again, family oriented. Unlike other nations, the French crèche is the focal point of celebration, and *la crèche* is created by the children. The crèche originated with descendants of Saint Francis, in Avignon, and by the sixteenth century the tradition was so widespread that it has prevailed to the present.

Enactment: While a teacher directs children to bring specific pieces for the crèche, the objects can be shown for the audience on a screen positioned above the children.

Narrator 13: [*Speaks of the French Yule log tradition which can be found in the bibliography.*]

Organ interlude comes after presentation.

F. Bethlehem

Narrator 14: Bethlehem is a Christian/Arab village, whose centuries of life are well preserved in structures, narrow streets, and jutting archways, all of which create an atmosphere felt, but little understood, by those who pilgrimage there to worship at Christmas.

Narrator 15: From the Jaffa Gate, on Christmas Eve, the Greek and Latin patriarchs lead separate but magnificent processions to the Basilica of the Nativity. As the bells peal out, worshipers kneel in the Grotto of the Manger as the mass intensifies in climax.

Narrator 16: [*Can speak of the Protestant celebration in the field of shepherds (check the bibliography).*]

The program can conclude with Narrator 17 telling the history of "O Little Town of Bethlehem" and everyone joining in singing the entire hymn.

Bibliography

Christmas: American Annual of Christmas Literature and Art, volume 25. Minneapolis: Augsburg Publishing House, pp. 32, 59.

Hole, Christine, *Christmas and Its Customs.* New York: M. Barrows & Company, Inc., 1957, pp. 30-31.

Krythe, Maymie R., *All About Christmas.* New York: Harper & Row, Publishers, 1954, pp. 24-26, 62, 77-80, 167-168.

Wernecke, Herbert H., ed., *Celebrating Christmas Around the World.* Philadelphia: The Westminster Press, 1962, pp. 59-66, 122-126.

_____, *Christmas Songs and Their Stories.* Philadelphia: The Westminster Press, 1957, pp. 11-12, 20, 25-26.

Yuletide in Many Lands. Boston: Lathrop, Lee & Shepard Company, 1916, pp. 37-38, 58-68, 123-126, 142-144.

Many of these books can be found in your local library. □

The Message of Christmas

The Community of Faith Celebrating Advent

● **by Thomas G. Bayes, Jr.**

What do—hammers, saws, flour, bread, felt cloth, a slide projector, a guitar, paint, and a Bible have in common?

Think about it for a moment. In the meantime, let me ask you another question.

What do—a three-year-old, a college student, a grandmother, a teenager, a single adult, a married couple, and a traditional family unit have in common?

The answer to both of these questions is the CELEBRATION OF ADVENT! A series of informal celebrations and industrious workshops served as a creative expression of our celebration of Advent at First Baptist Church. People of all generations shared common experiences and together discovered the very special meanings of Christmas.

No season of the year has more joy, hope, and excitement for Christians of all ages than does Advent. The season begins four Sundays before Christmas, and during this period we prepare for the celebration of Jesus' birth. Our preparation involves much anticipa-

The author is Minister of Education at the First Baptist Church, Madison, Wisconsin.

tion and reflection as we seek to respond to the wonders and beauty of this blessed event.

To emphasize the ageless nature of this season, the board of education designed a unique intergenerational experience in Christian education for our church school. All the classes, with the exception of the nursery and some of the two-year-olds, met together during the four Sundays of Advent.

Planning the Event

The board of education selected an intergenerational planning committee which was assigned the task of creating and developing an intergenerational learning experience. The committee set forth the following goals and objectives:

Goals:

As God's people, we seek to discover, experience, and celebrate the great joy and love of God's gift of love that was provided through the birth of his Son, Jesus. As we learn and share together, we hope that everyone will develop a new awareness and understanding of the meaning of Christmas within our church family.

Objectives:

(1) To help people discover the special meanings of Advent through shared experiences in our community of faith.

(2) To provide the opportunity for people of all ages to

    (*a*) get to know one another,

    (*b*) learn from each other,

    (*c*) have fun together.

(3) To provide a climate where we can build and strengthen relationships among the people of our church.

(4) To enable people to express creatively their own beliefs and thoughts about Christmas.

(5) To celebrate the love and joy of the Advent season.

Format

The committee decided that the first three Sundays would have three major focal points: *Advent Gatherings, Creating a Mosaic,* and *Advent Workshops.* The fourth Sunday would develop its own format.

The Advent Gatherings

To implement the objectives for our program, the planning committee decided on a format that would provide the necessary climate for interactions and learning to take place. The Advent gatherings were an informal time of fellowship at the beginning of the hour. In these sessions we learned and shared together in a worshipful and celebrative way.

I. "Christmas Is Special"

The purpose of the first session was to have each person share his/her own meaning of Christmas with one other person. As people arrived at Fellowship Hall, they were asked to make colorful name tags and introduce themselves to another person. While people were talking, our song leaders began to hum some carols. As people were seated, we sang some familiar Christmas carols.

The chairman of the board of education welcomed everyone and gave a brief synopsis of the overall Advent program. He then divided the people into groups of ten. Each group was given a piece of newsprint and a Magic Marker. The words "Christmas is special because . . ." were printed at the top of the paper. Each person was asked to share his/her response to the question with others in the group. Someone in the group was chosen to write the responses on the newsprint. When the sharing was completed, the sheets were taped to the wall so that the groups could share their ideas with others. We concluded this session of the program by singing "Hark! the Herald Angels Sing."

II. "The Coming of the Messiah"

The purpose of the second Sunday was to identify where Christ is needed and where Christ can be seen working in our world today. When people arrived, they were directed to a table covered with magazines and newspapers. People were instructed to find and cut out pictures of people who need help. These pictures were then taped to a posterboard entitled "We Need a Messiah Here."

A guitarist led us in the singing of hymns. The lights were turned down; and then, as he began to sing "O Come, O Come, Emmanuel," slides of people who need help were projected onto a large screen. (These included pictures of people who were ill, lonely, hungry.)

Our resource person for the morning taught us about the meaning of the word "Messiah" and what it meant to the people who lived in Israel at the time of Jesus' birth. (Background material was adapted from Griggs's *Teaching and Celebrating Advent.*) She then asked for everyone to help her sing "Joy to the World." Another series of slides showed pictures of Jesus and his ministry to the different needs of many people. The last slide focused on the manger scene. We then stood and sang "Away in a Manger." As we were ready to leave, we were challenged to follow Jesus' example and help someone during the Advent season.

III. "The Meaning of Gifts"

The third Sunday centered on the theme of "giving," in hopes that we would see that one of the greatest gifts we can receive is that of love. After our opening activities, each person was asked to find a partner and share his/her response to the question "What is the most special gift you have ever received?" This initiated some lively discussion. Some people shared their responses with the entire group. The leader reminded us that many of our most prized gifts are often gifts of love.

A brief introduction of the book *The Giving Tree* by Shel Silverstein was shared, and slides of the book were shown as it was being read. The children responded enthusiastically to the pictures and to the story. We concluded by singing "We Three Kings."

The use of banners in praising God is an ancient tradition of the church.

Baking gingerbread men to share with friends

Creating a Mosaic

The creating of our mosaic began some time before Advent. A high school youth had drawn a picture of the manger scene. The picture was color-coded with various colors of construction paper. The paper was then cut into hundreds of minute pieces.

After the Advent gatherings each Sunday, many people would help in the composition of the mosaic. The mosaic depicted the manger scene with Joseph, Mary, the baby Jesus, a wise man, and a shepherd.

The mosaic symbolized our common bond, and our efforts in creating it reflected the work of our entire church school community!

The Advent Workshops

A series of creative workshops met consecutively for the first three Sundays. They immediately followed the Advent gatherings and the work on the mosaic. Each workshop was designed to involve people of all ages in an enjoyable learning experience. Every workshop was to include: (a) an activity that would allow for interaction; (b) religious and educational content. The following workshops were chosen for our program:

Baking Workshop—This workshop focused on the fun and sharing of the Christmas season. People baked bread, ornament-shaped cookies, and gingerbread men that could be *shared* with friends and families or given to people in a convalescent home.

Banner Workshop—The use of banners in praising God is an ancient tradition of the church. In this workshop, banners told in symbols and in words the Good News that Christ is born.

Caroling Workshop—We discovered some of the history behind the traditional carols and joined in the fun of singing carols that were both familiar and new to us.

Making Christmas Gifts—The purpose of this group was to establish a real "work" shop in preparing toys and games for gifts during the Christmas season. The repaired and refurbished toys were given to the Dane County Social Service for distribution during Christmas.

Christmas Crafts—People had the opportunity to make family decorations or handmade gifts that could be given to neighbors or friends. Two craft workshops were available on each Sunday. Some of the crafts included an Advent wreath, a clothespin crèche, yarn decorations, etc.

Christmas Through the Great Masterpieces—This workshop was a slide presentation of the Christmas story as told through art, featuring some of the great masterpieces of the world.

Biblical Workshops—Studies were developed on the scriptural accounts of Jesus' birth. The first Sunday was entitled "The Christmas Story," and the last two were "Messiah—Hope for the World." (These were adapted from Griggs's book *Teaching and Celebrating Advent.*)

The Fourth Sunday

The purpose of the fourth Sunday was to bring a joyous and celebrative closure to our Advent program.

Fellowship Hall had been transformed into an actual learning center. The room itself characterized the excitement of this season. Displays of each of the workshops were located in various parts of the room. One could see tables covered with toys and games; banners were hanging all around the room; the aroma of baked bread filled Fellowship Hall.

As people talked together, music began playing. Our pianist played carols as people asked for them. When we had finished singing, the entire group responded to a request from the chaplain of the Dane County Jail; he had asked that some 150 Christmas cards be made for those inmates who would be spending Christmas Day in jail.

People earnestly and enthusiastically began work on the cards. They seemed to be working a little harder to make "these" cards just a little "more" special. As people finished their cards, they offered them as gifts of love. Then everyone's attention was immediately drawn to the work that was being done on the mosaic. Some of the children were determined to finish the mosaic before the end of the hour. People began to work frantically. The momentum began to build, and as the mosaic was completed, a loud roar went up. The mosaic was beautiful! What a sense of accomplishment!

People began to take a final look at some of the displays. Then everyone was seated for a very special film, *The Coming of Christ,* an exquisitely beautiful portrayal of the story of Jesus' birth. The movie reminded us that all the experiences of learning and sharing during the past weeks had prepared us for the coming again of Christ at Christmas.

After singing "Silent Night," we concluded our celebration by giving thanks to God for his greatest gift of love and, as his people, affirmed that

Christ *has come* into our world,
Christ *is coming* into our lives,
Christ *will come* in fulfillment of a hope
for a new world of peace and love. *   □

* Advent affirmation by Don Griggs

One group repaired and refurbished toys for distribution by a social service organization.

ADVENT'S PRICE TAG

A Potpourri of "Gift Ideas" for Junior Highs

• **by Mary Ellen Ton**

Advent is one of those times of which it can be said, "You get out of it what you put into it." A teacher is limited only by the amount of time he or she is willing to invest in junior highs during the Advent season. Some of the activities I am going to suggest will take a huge gift of time—a precious commodity during the hustle and bustle of Christmastime. You will have to decide how costly your gift will be. So here we go—my gift to you; if you catch a spark, pass it on.

First, two suggestions for the teacher who wants to give an *extravagant* gift.

Discover "The Bakerwoman," a musical allegory on the life of Christ.[1] Mary is the bakerwoman who bakes the bread (Jesus) in the oven (her womb), having received the grain of wheat from God. Here are some delightful activities to be built around this theme.

Few kids today have had the fun of baking bread. Maybe you yourself haven't. (Don't turn this off if you are a male. My dad baked all the bread in our home.) Naturally, this will involve more than one hour in class.

Mary Ellen Ton is a church school-teacher in Evansville, Indiana.

That's where the gift of time comes in. Begin by introducing the song to the group. Move into mixing and kneading the dough, giving everyone a chance to help. If you choose to do this on Sunday, the bread can rise during the worship service. Then several alternatives can be enjoyed. Spend some time now learning the song and talking about the innuendoes. Using the Index in *Good News for Modern Man,* the group might discover all it can about "bread" in the New Testament. Be sure to "experience" the smell of the bread as it bakes. This activity culminates in eating and enjoying the bread together. This would be an appropriate time to celebrate the Lord's Supper. Perhaps the group or a small committee could plan how this might be done while the bread bakes.

Many other ideas can be used with this theme—for example, banners and/or posters incorporating the symbolism of "bread." Unusual and attractive banners can be made from bread wrappers sewn together with a "jump-out" phrase, such as "Wonder Bread" cut out of felt or construction paper and glued on to the wrappers. Many interesting pictures of bread and word slogans are readily available in magazine advertisements which can be lifted out for posters. A game can be played having teams find as many references to "bread" in the hymnbook as they can. Either by themselves or with parents' help, the junior highs might be encouraged to bake bread at home to be shared with a friend or shut-in. Be sure they include a copy of the song. The kids may discover firsthand what it means to share the bread of life with someone. There are many recipes for simple, quick breads that even a junior high boy can easily handle. An all-church "Bread Night" might be sponsored by the class, asking everyone to bring his or her favorite kind of bread to be shared. The banners and posters could be displayed.

Here is another activity that could be shared with any number of groups within the church. (Aren't many of them looking for a Christmas program?) Slide pictures can be taken throughout the whole process of bread making. Junior highs are capable of doing this with just a little guidance in planning. Help them think through the procedure first and decide what pictures would best help to tell the story of the "Bakerwoman." These can then be interspersed with slides of the Nativity and other scenes that fit into the context of the song. The young people could "pose" for these, find available slides at church or a nearby film rental agency, or make slides of existing pictures found in teachers' kits. Let them use their imaginations. They might like to think of ways to make the slides "old-fashioned." For example, the girls might want to wear bicentennial-style dresses and caps while mixing the bread; a brick fireplace can be set up so that it appears as if the bread is baking there. It might be fun to contrast the old and the new: to show the birth scene in the stable and, with the help of a nurse or doctor friend, a picture of a modern delivery room. Showing the slides while listening to the song, learning the song and singing it while the slides are viewed a second time, a display of the banners and posters, maybe some bread to share, and the enthusiasm of a group of junior highs sharing their "gift" can provide a very meaningful experience for other members of the church family.

Through these activities the junior highs should experience firsthand that the "bread that God gives is he who comes down from heaven and gives life to the world" (John 6:33, TEV). Advent is the time to reflect on the meaning of his coming. They will be both "receivers" of life as they participate in the learning and fun of these events and "givers" as they share it with others. Advent is the time to grow in understanding of what it means to be a giver and a receiver of God's love.

Discover the "Chrismon" Tree. If your church is not acquainted with this custom, the junior high class could make the introduction this year. The time to start on this project is NOW. Chrismons are monograms for Christ. They are simply constructed out of Styrofoam and trimmings and when used as ornaments on the church Christmas tree speak a message all their own.[2] The young persons in your class can gain a significant amount of Bible knowledge as they join in making the Chrismons, discovering in the process the meaning of each one. In our church, one Sunday night in Advent becomes the time to "hang the Chrismons." The entire service is planned around this theme, and all present, young and old, participate as they hang the Chrismon of their choice on the tree. Junior highs can plan and execute this meaningful event for the whole church.

In a church where Chrismons are being introduced for the first time, the class might begin to work on the first Sunday of Advent making a few simple monograms which could be hung during the morning or evening service. Each week different Chrismons could be added as they are made, sharing the meaning as part of the worship service. Perhaps extra time during the week could be taken to construct some of the more elaborate and intricate symbols. This is one of the most meaningful traditions in our church. Most of your junior highs are probably church members, but they seldom have the opportunity to make a significant contribution to the life of the church family. This can be one of those happenings. See if you can work it out with your pastor. If it simply will not fit in the schedule, don't give up. Have the tree in your own room or fellowship hall and invite others to share before and/or

after church. Try it—you'll be glad you did!

Now for some ideas for the teacher looking for a *medium-cost* gift.

Discover the History and Tradition of Advent. Two excellent resources are: "Lord, Come" by John and Mary Harrell[3] and "Teaching and Celebrating Advent in Home and Church" by Patricia and Donald Griggs.[4] "Lord, Come" is a kit, complete with filmstrip, record, pictures, and study guide. My group particularly enjoyed making a "Chi Rho" as they learned about it through this study. "Teaching and Celebrating Advent" is a treasure box full of ideas for Advent use. There are some further suggestions for utilizing the "Lord, Come" kit, too. You will find both study and activity material, with a particularly good section for junior highs on the Messiah and a comparative study of the Christmas story as told in Matthew and Luke. Since both of these resources are multi-age media, your board of Christian education might consider purchasing them to have available for the entire church school.

Discover New Resources. A "Do-Your-Own-Thing" session or two during Advent is a welcome change from a curriculum-centered approach. Make as many resources as you can get your hands on available to your class, and let students make their own discoveries. Many churches have a collection of filmstrips (teachers' kits from *all* ages). Have some in the room and let the kids do their own projecting and script reading. Other good resources are materials to make minibanners (burlap, felt scraps, trimmings, etc.), books of Christmas stories, records, some quizzes on the Christmas story, or crossword puzzles (your own or from the Griggs resource).

Do they know about the Jesse tree? "The Twelve Days of Christmas Kit"[5] has an enabling resource they can use on their own. Provide a big, bare branch and watch the Jesse tree blossom.

Make up a batch of cookie dough the night before, scout out a portable oven, and junior highs will gladly fill the room with the "smell of Christmas."

How about a big, shallow box, some potting soil, sand, water, artificial or real greenery, straw, moss, and all the figures from a standard crèche set? I had five boys spend one entire morning constructing their own Nativity scene.

Have water paints and an easel available and suggest that students paint the one thing they would most like to say about Christmas. These paintings could decorate your room or be moved into a hallway to be shared with others.

Well, that's enough to get you started! Add your own ideas and take off. What will they learn? You can't measure the learning which this type of free activity brings. I can best tell you how I feel about it by sharing the prayer I offer before 9:30 A.M: "Lord, I have used my imagination and time to collect all this stuff and set up this room; others have created some of the resources; please use these gifts to speak to these kids you and I love."

And, Finally, Some Ideas for the Teacher Whose Schedule Is More Than Full Already. If you are a teacher with only a *mite* to give, you might choose to invest it in an exploration of the feelings of Mary and Joseph as they were caught up in the Christmas event. This not only can give a clearer insight into the whole meaning of Advent but also can communicate that it is still okay to envision marriage and family as goals. As junior highs look closely at Mary and Joseph, they can see how their early religious training, their sensitivity to God's activity in their lives, and their love and trust in each other enabled God to work through them to enter his creation in a unique way. Here is how you might get at this:

1. List those things the group already knows about Mary/Joseph.

2. Use the Index in *Good News for Modern Man* to make new discoveries.

3. What kind of person was this man/woman? Compose a character sketch.

4. Use modern writers to embellish understanding and imagination.[6]

5. How do you think they felt: Mary telling her parents and Joseph about her pregnancy? Joseph and her parents hearing this news? Mary in a barn giving birth? Joseph with her?

6. What do you think is the most important thing about this man/woman?

7. Why do you think God was able to work in their lives in this way?

8. Mary and Joseph's "claim to fame" is their role in parenting Jesus. Among all the goals we may have for our lives, parenting is still a worthy one and deserving of our best effort. The choices and decisions now being made by junior highs can be an important influence on their roles both as marriage partners and as parents.

Have you heard anyone say yet, "Oh, now, Christmas is on Sunday this year"? You probably will. Why not look on it as a unique opportunity? With the quiet loveliness of Christmas Eve still fresh and the excitement of the morning bursting out of its seams, what better time is there to celebrate together? This is the perfect time to zero in on a feeling level. The climate has been created for you—build on it. Here are two approaches that might be "just right" for you.

(1) Set the scene for relaxation. Some soft Christmas music and hot chocolate will go a long way to create that atmosphere. Have paper and pencils available for those who may want them as you gather together. Ask them to think quietly about the past twenty-four hours—the people they saw, the things they did, the different feelings they had. (They may want to jot some ideas down.) Continue by suggesting that they zero in on one particular happening: what went on, who else was involved, what did those others do, what did they themselves do, what feelings did they have? What word or short phrase best describes what the event meant to you? (This may be how you "felt" about it.) List their words and phrases on chalkboard or newsprint. Share in this experience yourself, and lead the way from a feeling level. Your own honesty will ease the way for them. Discuss the list: What does it say to you about the meaning of Christmas?[7] I can't say what your kids will make of it. Mine saw that almost all the words involved interaction with other persons. For them this meant that Christmas had a lot to do with being close to someone in special ways. We concluded that experiencing and sharing love was a special gift of Christmas. Some are ready to receive this "gift," and some are not. We then listened to the reading "Two Lonely People" from *Creative Brooding*[8] by Robert Raines.

(2) The second method utilizes a series of thought-provoking questions in a somewhat lighter vein and, therefore, turns the morning into a "fun" experience. This proceeds on the theory that even youth have "childhood" memories and enjoy remembering and sharing them. Use any or all of these as conversation starters: What is the very first Christmas you remember? What are some special things your family *always* does at Christmas? Is there one particular gift that you especially remember receiving? Is there some special gift that you either planned or helped plan for someone else? What gives you "warm" feelings at Christmas? My students discovered something in this session on which I hadn't counted. As they told about the gift they had received and the one they had given, one of those "Ah ha!" insights came about. They realized they had as much or more fun giving as getting. That's a big learning for anybody, much less for twelve- and thirteen-year-olds. We listened to "Barrington Bunny."[9] Barrington shares his unique gift—"Being warm and furry and able to hop." Each of us wrote on a piece of paper the unique gift we felt we had and with whom we might like to share it. These were very personal, and no one wanted to share. Even I didn't. One of the junior high girls was embarrassed to have tears in her eyes. As she left the room, I simply commented, "Feeling deeply is also a gift." She smiled and went on to the water fountain. Two or three kids came back in the room, saying, "Thanks for the hot chocolate." I think they were trying to say, "Merry Christmas."

The "outside" of Christmas is obvious. All the outside wrappings are readily seen from October on. These are great and a part and parcel of our celebration. But it is the "inside" of Christmas that I am eager to experience along with my class. Each of these activities will aid in some way to get "inside the parcel," to explore the "gift" and what it can mean to us. From thinking about the mystery of the ancient prophecies to breaking bread together, from learning about some symbols of our faith to comparing the feelings of those persons caught up in the first Advent with our own feelings—no matter which way you choose to "undo the package," I believe you will get "inside" Christmas.

---

[1] "The Bakerwoman"—words and music available from Vanguard Music Corporation, 250 West 57th Street, New York, NY 10019. Record available from Avant Garde Records, Inc., same address. "Let Trumpets Sound" recorded by the Presbyterian Chancel Choir.

[2] A complete book of instructions for making and hanging the Chrismons is available from the Lutheran Church of the Ascension, 295 West Main Street, Danville, VA 24541.

[3] John and Mary Harrell, P.O. Box 9006, Berkeley, CA 94709.

[4] Griggs Educational Service, 1731 Barcelona Street, Livermore, CA 94550. $4.00.

[5] "The Twelve Days of Christmas Kit," The Liturgical Press, Collegeville, MN 56321.

[6] *God Speaks to Women Today* by Eugenia Price and *Two from Galilee* by Marjorie Holmes are two such resources.

[7] The ideas in this approach are adapted from *Faith Recycling* by David Thornton (available through Judson Book Stores).

[8] *Creative Brooding,* edited by Robert Raines (available through Judson Book Stores).

[9] *The Way of the Wolf* by Martin Bell (Seabury Press).   □

From Seed to Flower—

the growth of a Christmas program

by K. Aart and Martha Jean VanDam

"We came early, and we still couldn't sit together."

"Well, what did you expect with the enthusiasm that children and adults have shown for this program?"

"This is the largest crowd we've ever had in our church for any service."

"I don't get it! What was the appeal anyway?"

These were but a few of the remarks heard around the Whiting Memorial Baptist Church of Neenah, Wisconsin, after the program on Christmas Eve. That night we had seen the flowering of an idea that had begun as a tiny seed almost a year before.

At the January meeting of the board of Christian education someone mentioned a church that had used colored slides in its Christmas program. The pictures were of biblical scenes posed by church school pupils. They told one phase of the story of Christmas.

"It seems to me that such pictures could be taken weeks or months ahead of time to avoid the Christmas rush," remarked the church school superintendent who was still weary from all the holiday activities.

The pastor's face lighted up. "Yes, and the script could be tape-recorded beforehand, also. Then we wouldn't have to worry if someone got a sore throat or the measles at the last moment."

"But wouldn't that take the personal element out of the program?" asked the chairman of children's work.

Our chairman of adult work had a ready reply. "Oh, no! Are there any parents who do not like to see pictures of their children—particularly when the pictures are shown before a group? We'd just have to make certain that every child and young person in the church school would be in at least one of the pictures. Think of the grandparents who would be interested, too."

"We could still have each department sing a Christmas song," said the superintendent.

"Well, now, let's not get too hasty," spoke up the chairman of youth work, who is a successful attorney in our community and likes to see a thing from all sides before jumping into it. "Who is going to take all of these pictures, and where are we going to get a script to go with the slides?"

This church is blessed with a number of good

photographers, both amateur and professional. One was selected who works on the house organ of a local paper manufacturing company and is an active Baptist layman. He agreed to do the photographic work. The pastor's wife fell heir to the task of preparing a suitable script.

Thus, the seed of our Christmas program was planted and given its first watering. For the next few months its nurture was left to the scriptwriter. This proved to be a slow-growing "plant" that took months to germinate and to break through the surface. In our service the story of Christmas must jell in a scripturally true manner and yet be different. The writer wanted to utilize Old Testament prophecy concerning the coming of Christ. A narrative form was desired to hold the interest of the children.

The first sprout to appear was the idea of having a young lad, the innkeeper's servant boy, tell the story. He would be telling it to the village rabbi who had been out of town at a conference during most of the happenings. The rabbi would show doubt during most of the story; however, the facts would convince him. At the end he, too, would worship the young child.

After a couple of revisions a meeting was called of the superintendent (who would direct the production), the photographer, a church school teacher who had agreed to be in charge of costumes, the pastor, and his wife.

The script was ready for pruning and reshaping so that it might be a more suitable "plant." The servant boy became three children (two boys and a girl) in order to break up the longer speeches and to add interesting voice changes. This was important in a program that was to be entirely on slides and tape. Some small changes were also made.

Next, the story was studied to decide what pictures should be taken. The dialogue was combined to fit the respective pictures. These were numbered and listed on a separate sheet with appropriate descriptions. Corresponding numbers went into the manuscript. Then a list was made of all the characters, with suggestions regarding their costumes.

At a later meeting of the superintendent, the costumer, and the pastor's wife, plans were made for inviting every church school student up through the Senior High Department to participate.

Next, the costumer began to function. She had a few costumes on hand which could be used. One of the women's organizations gave money for the purchase of materials for additional costumes. With this and plenty of originality she went to work. The costumer proved to be a genius at concocting authentic-looking costumes out of items on hand or readily available. When a Halloween space helmet was touched up with aluminum paint and cut into a different shape, it became the headdress for a Roman soldier. When taken apart, a dime-store wig yielded many beards for men of ancient Palestine. Herod was resplendent in a white robe with a wide, purple cape. This was trimmed with white cotton to which small tufts of black fur from the collar of someone's cast-off coat were attached to give the impression of ermine.

Using the list of required slides, a tentative schedule was made for the various scenes to be photographed. All the pictures in which any one group, such as shepherds, would appear were to be taken at one time. Then a committee started contacting each child by phone to give the time and location for the picture or pictures he/she was to appear in. It was later agreed that a great deal of time and explaining could have been saved if a mimeographed letter had preceded the calls. When the participants came together, the script was carefully read, and the plan and purpose of the picture taking explained. Each person was thus helped to feel the character whom he/she was to represent.

It was time for "shoots" to appear (the "shooting" of the pictures). Some were taken out-of-doors, some in a barn, some in the photographer's studio, and others in the church—wherever a background could be found appropriate to the story. When the right setting was not available, some object that would symbolize the location was used. For example, a plain background with two candelabra was used for scenes in the temple.

The photographer worked like an artist to obtain the right groupings, expressions, and lighting for each picture. His consecrated Christian concern was evident in many of the properties, settings, and techniques which he used. Some of these were developed for this project. He took at least two shots, and usually more, of each scene. To bring the story up to present times, three pictures were taken of children today learning and worshiping in our church. These were taken on a Sunday morning and included those students who had been unable to be in any of the other pictures. Thus, the goal of having every church school pupil up through the youth department in at least one scene was realized.

The slides were completed before work on the tape was started. Voices for this part of the production were selected on the basis of reading ability and expression. These qualities were determined through trial recordings. In only two cases did the person pictured in a certain role also read that part. This helped to involve more people.

The recording was all done on one Saturday afternoon. All participants had copies of the script for at least a week previous. Since no memorizing was necessary, they had time to read the script several times to develop expression. We recorded the whole thing at one time and then let those who had read the script hear it as the slides were shown. This showed up the weak spots. It took two more tries before a reasonably good recording was obtained. More effort at this point would be worthwhile.

During all of the picture taking and tape recording, enthusiasm in the church family was mounting. Practically every family had someone in the program. By the middle of November it became apparent that the program would have to be presented twice in order to accommodate everyone who wished to see it.

The flowering of this two-blossomed "plant" was glorious to behold. Two services were scheduled: the first for Christmas Eve and a second for the Sunday evening after Christmas. The comments heard after those two occasions and since have made us thankful to the Lord, who surely helped us to plant and finally bring to flower our Christmas program □

'Christmastime with Our Person-on-the-Street'

by Elizabeth C. Strauss

CHARACTERS

MR. GIMMIE—a fat, sloppy man, carrying a Sears catalog.

GIMMIE GIMMIE—son of Mr. Gimmie, also fat and sloppy and loud, carrying a list headed "To Santa," six feet long.

MRS. BUSYBUSYBUSY—an obviously uptight woman, wearing tennis shoes, pulling a small shopper's cart behind her, and reading a list of things she must do; a bustle of activity and concern.

MR. BAH HUMBUG—a grouchy-looking old man in a long coat and hat, carrying a cane and a newspaper with which he hits small children and animals who get in his way. He walks slowly, slouching, and looks suspiciously out of the corner of his eye.

MADAME PARTY—an elegantly dressed woman; a social butterfly who walks and speaks in proper fashion.

MR. HARRY PRICE—a salesman with a friendly, but pushy, manner; always trying to sell, he sounds like a walking commercial. He carries a small artificial Christmas tree.

MS. IMA WARE—a college student, dressed in blue jeans and a poncho, having long hair and a back pack or shoulder bag, books on arm; a serious, pessimistic young woman.

ANNIE TUXIS—a fifth- or sixth-grade girl (or boy, Tommy), dressed in winter clothes, carrying a small bag of items.

MR. MIKE ASKUM (or MS. FRIEDA INQUIRE)—CBS newsperson* dressed in suit, overcoat, and hat, holding microphone and wearing a CBS button or sign on coat.

SETTING: On the sidewalk in front of a large department store window. (Taped Christmas music is heard softly in the background. It sounds tinny.)

COSTUMES: Winter coats, hats, and scarves. Carrying bundles, bags, or boxes. Also note specific items for each character, as outlined above.

SCENERY: A storefront built out of cardboard, having simply a window or doorway decorated for Christmas.

PROPS: Sign announcing the title of the play. Microphone and cord and an artificial Christmas tree.

The play begins with our newsperson interviewing Christmas shoppers in front of a department store.

*This lengthy part may be divided between two reporters.

MR. MIKE ASKUM: Well, here we are on this snowy, winter evening. We are standing in front of the Jordan Marsh Department Store in downtown Boston. With only four more shopping days until Christmas, the hustle and bustle of shopping is nearing its peak. Let's talk to a few of the people passing by tonight and find out what they think about this holiday season. Hello, sir—and you, sonny, Merry Christmas. Can you tell us what Christmas means to you?

MR. GIMMIE: Christmas! Wow, it's the best time of year! Do you see this catalog? I'm gonna get me everything in here that I want!

MIKE: Excuse me, sir, I didn't get your name. What is your name?

MR. GIMMIE: Gimmie, Mr. Gimmie. And this is my son, Gimmie Gimmie.

GIMMIE GIMMIE: Look what Santa's gonna give me! *(He holds up his long list.)*

MIKE: Uh, huh—OK—well, Seasons Greetings to you. *(Father and son hurry off.)* Well, isn't credit wonderful! Say, here comes a woman in a hurry. Excuse me, ma'am, could we have a moment of your time? Your name, please?

MRS. BUSYBUSYBUSY *(as she says each word, she makes hand movements to demonstrate the actions in a pantomiming fashion; speaks very quickly and out of breath):* Phew! I'm rolling, cutting, baking. I'm buying, boxing, wrapping. I'm writing, licking, mailing. I'm trimming, decorating, hanging. And now I'm shopping, buying, running—. *(She runs off stage.)*

MIKE: *(shouting after her):* Merry Christmas! *(More conversationally.)* I'm exhausted just thinking of all that. Hope she doesn't have a heart attack. Ah, here's a fellow who looks much more relaxed about the holiday season. Hello, sir, may I ask you your name?

MR. HUMBUG *(dully and dryly):* Yes.

MIKE: Uh, well then, what is your name? Speak right into here. *(Holding out the microphone.)*

MR. HUMBUG: Humbug.

MIKE: Humbug? Humbug. And your first name?

MR. HUMBUG: Bah. Bah Humbug!

MIKE *(a nervous chuckle):* Well, Mr. Humbug, would you mind telling us what all the Christmas festivities mean to you?

MR. HUMBUG: Yeck! Sickening! Worthless! Bothersome! Stupid! Expensive! Noisy! Wasteful! Nonsense! Criminal! Shameful! Frightening! Empty! Lonely! *(Quieter, slower, as he wanders off.)* Sad! No one. Empty. Lonely. Sad. No one—.

MIKE: Gee, I'm sorry you feel that way, sir. *(He calls*

Ms. Elizabeth Strauss is a fifth- and sixth-grade church school teacher at the First Baptist Church in Newton Centre, Massachusetts. She is also a speech pathologist.

after him.) Merry Christmas! *(He mumbles.)* Happy New Year. Oh, well, he must have someone—now here's a smart, happy-looking woman. Merry Christmas, ma'am. What is your name?

MADAME PARTY *(cheerfully):* Merry Christmas to you. I'm Madame Party. Haven't I met you somewhere before? Wasn't it at a cocktail party, or was it a tea? A reception? Anyway, you sure do look familiar.

MIKE: No, I'm afraid we've never met before. I'm *sure* I'd remember a woman as lovely as you! Tell me, what does Christmas mean to you, Madame Party?

MADAME PARTY *(excitedly):* Oh, well, today I'm in charge of the Women's Club Annual Christmas Tea. We all bake cookies and send what's left over from our tea to the starving children of India. And tomorrow evening we have a PTA Christmas Open House. And Tuesday we're having the neighbors in for a Christmas cocktail hour. And on Wednesday afternoon we have my husband's office party. Everyone brings a gift for the grab bag. Such fun! And then Wednesday night we have a Christmas buffet at the Murrays' to go to. And, of course, on Thursday there's the party—,

MIKE *(clears his throat):* Hm-hm. Yes, well it sounds like you're all partied up, Madame. Happy Holidays! *(She and he wave goodbye.)* Remember, don't drink when you drive, or drive when you drink, *(Mumbles.)* or whatever. *(In normal tone.)* Hello, sir, I see you've got a Christmas tree there. What does Christmas mean to you?

MR. PRICE: Harry Price is the name. Stop in at the Price Is Right anytime. Just two doors down from the Stop and Shop. Open twenty-four hours a day during the Christmas season. We've got *the most* beautiful artificial Christmas trees! All sizes. All shapes. All colors. Long or short needles. And to go with the tree—ornaments, tinsel, angels that glow in the dark, flickering colored lights, and a revolving rainbow spotlight! Everything to make your Christmas *the best* Christmas ever! And for your rooftop—more lights, a life-size Santa Claus and his eight reindeer. We've got it all at Price Is Right. Open twenty-four hours a day.

MIKE: Excuse me, Mr. Price, this is television, and we don't allow free advertising. Seasons Greetings to you just the same. *(He gently pushes MR. PRICE on down the street to get him to leave. A young woman has been watching MR. PRICE speak from the side of the stage. She approaches MIKE.)*

MS. IMA WARE: I'd like to say something to the TV viewers. My name is *Ms.* Ima Ware. I go to

"We sing Christmas carols."

"Excuse me, ma'am, could
we have a moment of your time?"

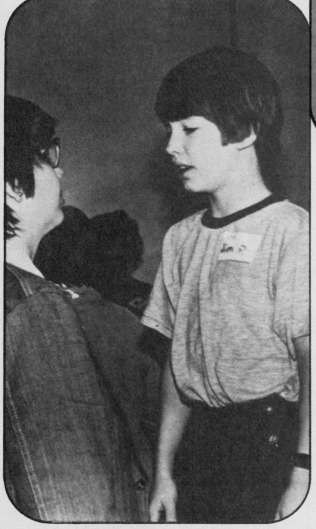

college here in Boston, and I'm aware that Christmas is a destructive force in our society. Christmas is only adding to our guilt trip. Like, it's hypocritical to eat turkey when 90 percent of the world is starving. Like, it's criminal to spend money on gifts when 50 percent of the people are on welfare. Like, it's a heavy scene, you know? I'm aware that it's cool to meditate. Why don't people just get it together and meditate on Christmas? Forget the turkey and the presents. *(She sits yoga-style at the edge of the stage, closes her eyes.)* Om-m-m.

MIKE: Freaky! Well, just enough time for one more Christmas conversation. Hello, young lady. Merry Christmas. What's your name?

ANNIE TUXIS: Annie Tuxis. Hi. *(She looks at the camera.)* Hi, Mom; hi, Dad. Hi, everybody.

MIKE: Annie, what does Christmas mean to you?

ANNIE TUXIS *(looks at the audience and speaks sincerely):* Well, to me Christmas is a time when all my family gets together. The house smells of good food. Everywhere there is Christmas cheer and a warm feeling of love. We sing Christmas carols. We read the story of Christ's birth. We thank God for sending his Son to earth. We all enjoy being together, eating together, and giving gifts to each other. I guess that's my idea of Christmas. *(She steps toward IMA WARE.)* Merry Christmas, Ima. Wanna come meditate at my house? We got a lot of good vibrations at my house. *(She bends down and picks up IMA'S books. The two girls walk off the stage together.)*

MIKE: Thank you and Merry Christmas, Annie. *(He looks at the audience.)* And Seasons Greetings. *(He walks off the stage.)*   □

END

CHRISTMAS HAS BEEN CANCELED

by **W. Barkley Butler, James L. Pike,** and the Junior High B. Y. F., First Baptist Church, Madison, Wisconsin

The following play is reprinted with permission from *Respond, Volume 2,* a program resource book for youth groups. The production of the play could prove to be an exciting and fun way of dealing with the meaning of Christmas in the lives of youth and adults.

PREPARATION

The stage is divided into two stages, right and left.

STAGE: On stage left, a family living room: fireplace with red stockings, couch, rug, lamp, pictures on walls, easy chair, and table. On stage right, a giant "television set" with cardboard and dials, risers for small choir.

PROPS: Red "Santa" hats for choir members; choir robes; a large sign which says "BULLETIN" for use with giant TV set; large Bible; and signs of a commercial Christmas for family living room. Bathrobes and slippers for family members. A bare Christmas tree; a manger and some greenery. (Maybe a record player.) Commercial Christmas cards (no mention of Jesus). A candle (wide and decorative). Two spotlights. (Stage manager should be in charge of lighting.)

CHARACTERS: Narrator, mother, father, four children, newscaster, piano player, and choir members.

CHRISTMAS HAS BEEN CANCELED

(As the play begins, the lights go down and the spotlight goes on the NARRATOR at a podium on the floor in front of stage left.)

NARRATOR: It's Christmas time again. Remember? It happens each December. Well—to tell the truth, they began it in late October this year: it seems to arrive earlier each year—sort of like the new cars. Anyhow, December is when it reaches its climax or really starts to get to you, depending on your point of view.

(Lights on family.)

This is the Williams family. They could live anywhere—New York, Chicago, San Francisco, but they happen to live here. Let's see how they're coming with their Christmas preparations. They ought to be about finished; there are only a few days left now.

Oh, dear! It looks as if they haven't even finished their Christmas cards.

SCENE: MOTHER and FATHER seated at card table doing Christmas cards, great stacks of envelopes, etc. The two younger children (use their real names) are playing on the floor.

MOTHER: Did you send Aunt Florence a Santa card or a Rudolph one, dear?

FATHER: What difference does it make?

MOTHER: Well, I don't want to send the same one to Cousin Millie. They live next door to each other, you know.

FATHER: *(sarcastically):* Yeah, that would be terrible. Say, where are those fifty-cent cards with the

* Reprinted from *Respond, Volume 2,* 1972. Reprinted with permission of Judson Press, Valley Forge, Pennsylvania.

gold lettering? I need one for my boss.

MOTHER: I used the last one for Pastor Gladhand.

FATHER: Well, we'll just have to get some more. Say, is the Sanders' party tomorrow night or Sunday?

MOTHER: Sunday, but we're going to the church family night, so we can't go.

FATHER: Miss the Sanders' party for a potluck supper with a bunch of screaming kids? Forget it! I can't stand potluck suppers.

MOTHER: Well, you'll stand this one. I promised Gloria Gladhand I would help. Besides, the kids look forward to getting a present from Santa. Jeremiah Smith is going to be Santa Claus again. He's always such a good one.

(GEORGE and MARY, the two older children, burst into the room, arguing and pushing each other.)

MARY: Mother, tell George he can't use the gold wrapping paper. He just messes it up, and I need it for your present.

GEORGE: She won't let me use any of the new paper. All I get is the stuff from last year's presents with Scotch tape all over it. What makes her think she's so great?

(Just then the two little children start fighting over a toy: one hits the other, who starts crying. GEORGE and MARY continue to argue over the paper.)

FATHER: Shut up! All of you. If you don't stop this fighting, I'll just take back all the presents and forget the whole thing. The way I feel right now, I wish Christmas were over and done with. I hate it!

MOTHER: Well, at least we agree on one thing. I'd never miss it if they would just skip Christmas.

LITTLE BOY *(in panic):* Isn't there going to be a Christmas? I want to get a fire truck and a ray gun and a space suit and—

LITTLE GIRL: Am I going to get my doll, Mommy? Am I? Huh?

GEORGE: Yeah, Dad, and don't forget those skis I want, and the boots and jacket.

MARY: And that dress and sweater. I'll die if I don't get those.

MOTHER: All right! You're getting on my nerves. Why don't you turn on the television? It's time for the "Goodmonth" Santa Christmas Special.

(She goes out and returns with popcorn and soda while one of the children turns on the TV.)

How about stringing some more popcorn for the tree? I think the Holiday Singers and Dancers are on tonight.

(The lights go down on the family and half up on the TV with the NARRATOR'S light going on, too. The choir, dressed in Santa hats, sings one verse of "Santa Claus Is Coming to Town" or some other song.)

NARRATOR (*piano plays softly during narration*): Sound familiar? Sort of brings that dull December ache back to your head? I wonder why it seems so natural when we play the parts ourselves? Well, that chorus sounds good and the song is familiar. Why don't we all join them and sing along.

(*The lights go way down on the family and all the way up on the TV, and the NARRATOR directs the audience to the end of the song.*)

CHOIR MEMBER: And now listen as the choir sings their own rendition of that famous Christmas carol, "Rudolph, the Red-nosed Reindeer."

(*The choir starts on "Rudolph, the Red-nosed Reindeer," which is interrupted at the point of "Santa came to say. . . .")*

NEWSCASTER (*reading and pushing his way through the TV singers*): We interrupt this Christmas special to bring you a news bulletin. This bulletin has just been received. Christmas has been canceled. We repeat. Christmas has been canceled. This is all we know at this time. We will broadcast more information as we receive it. We do not know the reason for this announcement. We do know that all Christmas preparations are to cease immediately. No trees, parties, decorations, cards, or presents are allowed. We repeat. Christmas has been canceled. No trees, parties, decorations, cards, or presents are allowed.

(*The lights begin to come up on the family, who are looking very upset and surprised.*)

In keeping with this order, we cannot continue the special you were watching. WFBC will now leave the air. We will return to the air at 9:00 P.M. E.S.T. for the regularly scheduled program, "The Avengers."

(*TV lights off and choir leaves. Lights all the way up on family. Everyone staring at the TV with look of amazement. Then tears from the little ones, confusion, etc.*)

LITTLE GIRL: Did the man say there won't be Christmas, Mommy?

LITTLE BOY: Does that mean Santa won't come, Dad? Does it?

GEORGE: Does that mean I won't get my skis? They can't do that, can they?

FATHER: Well, at least we don't have the tree yet.

MOTHER: What will we do with all these cards we haven't mailed yet? And what am I going to do with six pumpkin pies?

FATHER: And I just bought a plastic Santa Claus that lights up for the lawn. What do I do with that?

MOTHER (*to FATHER*): What does it mean, dear?

How can they cancel Christmas? I mean, it's sort of a relief in a way, but just to do it without asking anybody. Shouldn't we have voted on it or something? It's sure going to be hard on the kids.

FATHER: Well, I don't know; I guess we'll get along without it. We can save the kids' presents for their birthdays. They get everything they want anyway, and we do too, for that matter. Maybe—

GEORGE: Dad, how can they just say there isn't any Christmas? There's always been Christmas, hasn't there? Why stop it now? If they didn't want it, why let it get started? How did it get started, anyhow?

(*Action stops, light comes on for NARRATOR.*)

NARRATOR: I know what you're all thinking. Don't be ridiculous. You're putting me on, right? Nobody could be so dumb as not to know how Christmas got started. Especially nobody coming to a church Christmas play. We all know, right? Of course, we won't ask what your kids would think Christmas was all about if all they knew was from watching you go through one. But we all know, don't we? Well, no matter, these people really know, too. They almost have forgotten, but they know. The parents are getting ready to explain it now. Want to listen in just to be sure they're getting it right?

(*Lights off on NARRATOR and action resumes in play.*)

FATHER: How did Christmas get started? Didn't you learn that story in Sunday school about shepherds and kings coming to give presents to a baby? It's all in the Bible.

MOTHER: I remember when we used to go to Grandpa's when I was a little girl. We would sit by the fireplace, and Grandpa would read that story out of the family Bible. That was so long ago. But Christmas was so much fun and so relaxed and—it was even—inspirational. It's so different now, or it was till a few minutes ago. I'd forgotten all about that.

LITTLE BOY: Would you read us that story about how Christmas all started?

MARY: Yeah, I never thought much about it until now when they canceled it.

FATHER: Where is that old Bible? (*It is on an end table, covered with dust. He blows off the dust and asks his wife to find the story.*)

MOTHER: Where is it now? (*Looking through book.*) Oh, yes, here it is with Grandpa's bookmark.

FATHER (*reads. Soft music in background. TV lights*

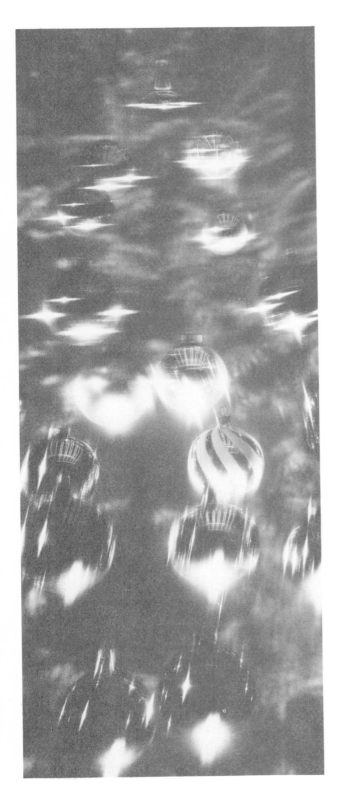

come up and family lights soften. Father reads while the choir sings softly in background and comes up louder to finish each song after his reading has stopped.):

Luke 2:1-7 *(Choir sings first verse of "The Virgin Mary Had a Baby Boy" or "Silent Night.")*

Matthew 2:1-2 *(Choir sings "We Three Kings.")*

Luke 2:8-14 *(Choir sings "While Shepherds Watched Their Flocks" or "The First Noel.")*

Matthew 2:9-12 *(Choir sings rest of "The Virgin Mary Had a Baby Boy" or "Away in a Manger.")*

MOTHER: And that's how Christmas got started. Funny how we'd forgotten that in all the Christmas rush. Maybe that's why Christmas got canceled. We were thinking of all the popcorn and parties and presents and forgot all about the real meaning.

LITTLE GIRL: What happened to the baby?

FATHER: After the wise men gave him gifts, he grew up; and when he was a man, Jesus gave his life that there might be love and peace for all men. That is the greatest gift of all.

MARY: And that's why we give presents?

GEORGE: And Christmas isn't getting presents, really; it's giving them.

MOTHER: That's right. We give to others, not just presents, but more important, ourselves, our love, because God gave himself to us. Maybe Christmas will really be Christmas if we think of it that way.

(Choir begins singing "O Holy Night" or some other carol. Lights go down on family and up on the NARRATOR and chorus.)

NARRATOR: Maybe Christmas will really be Christmas. Who knows? For many people the real Christmas was canceled long ago—not for lack of interest, or lack of time, or lack of bread, not even by a TV news bulletin. For them Christmas was canceled by a preoccupation with all of the "busywork" of the holiday season. It's just too bad the Christ part of Christmas gets lost in the shuffle.

(Choir sings "I Wonder as I Wander" with guitars. Prayer by NARRATOR.)

□

CELEBRATIONS

by Claire J. Hill

We might be among those who say, "All of life is a celebration," but most of us value the times which are special to our family or church. Certain holidays are traditionally observed in our church school classes, and rather than detract from these observances, let's be open to some new/different types of holiday celebrations. It takes little imagination to light birthday candles on a cardboard cake or pass out stockings of candy. How well do these rituals say how we really feel about these occasions? We want our children and friends to experience a sense of awe and excitement at these events.

Sharon Cadwallader, in her book *In Celebration of Small Things* (Houghton Mifflin Company), has a chapter on the restoration of ritual. She defines ritual as "acts or rites growing out of years or even generations of common beliefs and customs . . . , ceremonies to observe religious faith, to commemorate past privation and hard times; and . . . festivities that memorialize the times of good fortune—all acts that hold a family or society together."

Ms. Cadwallader speaks of "redesigning" our ways of celebrating. If we pursue this concept in the light of our Christian faith, we might want to ask ourselves if we can best observe Thanksgiving Day by gorging ourselves, or remember Christ's birth by overspending money on junk, or celebrate the resurrection by hiding eggs in the piano on Easter morning at church school.

The birthday of a five-year-old is an event worth celebrating, and we want to say to that child, "You are unique." Whether acting from the position of teacher or parent, it is necessary to know what would help that particular child know that he/she is a special person.

The Alternate Celebrations Catalog points to some very creative and meaningful ways to play out these acts of love in our church and family life. The thrust is away from gifts involving expense instead of time and thought. It is toward nutrition (as well as taste) in party food instead of teeth-spoiling sweets; a giving of self in the act of making the gift instead of buying it. An emphasis is on traditions that begin when the family is young and children small. A good illustration of these points is a young boy who prepared for Christmas, 1975, by painstakingly making original gifts for each member of his family (aunts, uncles, cousins). This was a year-long activity which involved wood and nails, crayons and paper, thought and imagination.

Pablo Casals said, "You are unique, you are one of a kind. In all the world there is no one exactly like you." That is worth celebrating. □

Ms. Hill is associated with the Mansfield Public Library in Mansfield, New Jersey

• by Robert Earl Slaughter

A Cavalcade of Carols

A Christmas Worship Service Centered Around the Christmas Carols

This service was developed and used by the author on the third Sunday of Advent at the Roselawn Community Baptist Church, Cincinnati, Ohio.

BACKGROUND FOR TODAY'S WORSHIP

"And suddenly there was with the angel a multitude of the heavenly host praising God and saying,

> 'Glory to God in the highest,
> and on earth peace among men
> with whom he is pleased!'"
> (Luke 2:13-14).

"The origin of the word 'carol' is obscure; some say it is related to the 'circle' or 'ring' dance from carolare (meaning "to sing") and originally denoting 'a dance accompanied by singing.' In early religious rites, worshipers joined hands and danced in a circle as they sang together. Certain sources believe that 'carol' may be derived from the Greek word for 'flute player,' referring to the musician who accompanied the singing of the dancing group.

"At Christmas, A.D. 129, Bishop Telesphorus of Rome urged his people to gather in the churches and sing the 'Gloria in Excelsis Deo,' or the 'Angels Song.'

The Reverend Slaughter is Minister of the Roselawn Community Baptist Church in Cincinnati, Ohio.

Saint Jerome also mentions the use of carols in the fifth century. Several Latin hymns celebrated the holy birth, including one of the eighth century, 'Christ Is Born! Tell Forth His Name!'

". . . our carols really date from the fifteenth century, for then the minds of men were beginning to be freed from the old period when the Church had 'suppressed the dance and the drama, denounced communal singing, and warred against the tendency of the people to disport themselves in church on the festivals.'"

Maymie R. Krythe

THE PRELUDE "Noels for Organ" Daquin-Biggs (1694–1771)

THE LIGHTING OF THE CANDLE OF LOVE

The Lesson
The Reading
The Lighting of the Candle

INTRODUCTION TO THIS SERVICE

There's a song in the air! Carols, carols everywhere! The air is filled with carols all around the globe. Every radio station, every TV channel, the piped-in music in stores of every kind, our car tapes all carry Christmas carols in traditional renditions and other beats. This can be a mixed blessing. If it serves to spread the best news ever of the greatest Gift, it is good. But if it makes the message and the melodies so tiresome as to tarnish

their value through overexposure or misuse, then the result can be bad.

Within the Christian fellowship we need to use the carols in every possible sacred setting and to see their glorious message in light of faith, hope, and love. The carols in any hymnal may be used to tell the Good News, even as this simple pattern from *Christian Worship* (Judson Press) will illustrate.

Let everyone join in "jovial singing," for that is the style and mood for carol singing! Carols bring joy as they tell stories, present theological beliefs, praise God and Jesus, and present a call for commitment.

THE PROCESSIONAL

"Angels, from the Realms of Glory" (No. 192)

THE INVOCATION AND THE LORD'S PRAYER

THE GLORIA PATRI

THE WELCOME TO WORSHIPERS

Registration of all worshipers
Welcome to guests

WORSHIP THROUGH TITHES AND OFFERINGS

The Sentences
The Prayer
The Organ Offertory
    "I Heard the Bells on Christmas Day"
The Doxology

THE HOLY SCRIPTURE—Your own selection

In the "Cavalcade of Carols" which follows, the page number in the Christian Worship *hymnal (Judson Press) is given for each carol. You can, of course, find the carols in other hymnals or songbooks.*

Depending on the time available, you may vary the use of the carols. Some may be sung by the congregation (all verses or only the ones mentioned); some may be sung by a choir, a soloist, or a group;

some may be read, with the congregation following the words in the hymnal; or the leader may just refer to the carol and tell of its special significance.

"A CALVACADE OF CAROLS"
I. The Promise

* "O Come, O Come, Emmanuel" (No. 182) has the oldest carol melody and text in the hymnal and carries the message of the promise of God to send full salvation to his chosen, "captive Israel."
* "Watchman, Tell Us of the Night" (No. 183) asks the watchman to look for signs of his coming, the "promised day of Israel."
* The fourth verse of "It Came upon the Midnight Clear" (No. 191) reminds us that the Advent was "by prophetbards foretold."
* Verse two of "Lo, How a Rose E'er Blooming" (No. 194) proclaims "Isaiah 'twas foretold it."

II. The Place

* The most familiar of all the "place" carols is "O Little Town of Bethlehem" (No. 184).
* Gracious and urgent is the invitation to take the annual journey with the shepherds in the third stanza of the carol "Angels We Have Heard on High" (No. 187), where the author beckons, "Come to Bethlehem, and see Him whose birth the angels sing."
* Recalling the lineage and heritage of Jesus, we know that the birth town had special significance as the third verse of the carol "While Shepherds Watched Their Flocks by Night" (No. 185) reminds us: "'To you, in David's town this day, is born of David's line, the Saviour, who is Christ the Lord.'"
* The star was the guide to the town. It drew near and "o'er Bethlehem it took its rest," according to the fourth stanza of "The First Noel, the Angel Did Say" (No. 197).
* "Born a King on Bethlehem's plain" are the words attributed to those kings who came to acknowledge his lordship over the mighty. This is found in the familiar kings' carol "We Three Kings of Orient Are" (No. 204) in the second verse.

III. The People

* Heralds of the Coming—angels—are in so many joyful songs. One of the very best of these bids us "Hark! the Herald Angels Sing" (No. 189).
* Mary and Joseph are noted affectionately in verse four of one of the carols already mentioned, "Angels We Have Heard on High" (No. 187).
* Shepherds are in so many of the carols but no more wonderfully than in "While Shepherds Watched Their Flocks by Night" (No. 185) and in the first verse of "The First Noel, the Angel Did Say" (No. 197).

THE ANTHEM "O Beloved Shepherds" Hammerschmidt (1612-1675)

- Of course, Jesus is in the carols, for they are about his coming; but no place do we find reference to him more tender than in the one carol children love the most: "Away in a Manger, No Crib for His Bed" (No. 199).
- The other best-known people in the Christmas story are the kings, whose well-known carol is "We Three Kings of Orient Are" (No. 204).

What a shame it is that we have no well-known or often used carol about the innkeeper! Such mention as we have is in cantatas or in hymnals not in general use.

IV.   The World, Nature

- Light and darkness are prominent parts of religious expression, and the most beloved of all the carols tells us that though it is night, "all is calm, all is bright. . . . Darkness flies, all is light. . . . Son of God, love's pure light. . . ." All this and more is to be found in "Silent Night, Holy Night" (No. 188).
- The rose of Sharon is remembered in the lovely lullaby carol "Lo, How a Rose E'er Blooming" (No. 194).
- Another lullaby reminds us of the song in the air, the mother's prayer, the baby's cry, and a star that "rains its fire" in the text of "There's a Song in the Air!" (No. 198).
- One of the lesser known and seldom sung carols tells us that the message came "Calm on the List'ning Ear of Night" (No. 201).

THE ANTHEM "Softly the Night" Italian Carol arr. by Theron Kirk

V.   The Response, Then and Now

- Joy and rejoicing were and are the right response to God's great Good News. "All My Heart This Night Rejoices" (No. 186), says the carol in its title and in its words.
- "Good Christian Men, Rejoice" (No. 193) bids us to "rejoice with heart and soul and voice!"
- We are invited to cry out and shout, "Joy to the World! The Lord Is Come" (No. 190) in the singing of this carol.
- One of the neglected carols, "Hush, All Ye Sounds of War" (No. 195), pleads that the Prince of Peace may see his hopes fulfilled.
- "Come and worship, worship Christ, the newborn King" is the open invitation to respond in worship through the carol "Angels, from the Realms of Glory" (No. 192).
- Through the familiar "O Come, All Ye Faithful"

(No. 205) ring the words "O come, let us adore Him, Christ, the Lord!"
- Do not delay in this homage is the message of the text of "What Child Is This, Who, Laid to Rest" (No. 200); rather, "Haste to bring Him laud, the Babe, the Son of Mary."
- Good as it is to rejoice, worship, and praise, the last carol in this suggested Cavalcade invites and challenges us to *live* our praise. In the singing of "As with Gladness Men of Old" (No. 196), the fourth stanza holds particular significance as we consider our commitment:

> "As they offered gifts most rare
> At that manger rude and bare,
> So may we with holy joy,
> Pure, and free from sin's alloy,
> All our costliest treasures bring,
> Christ, to Thee, our heavenly King. Amen."

THE RECESSIONAL CAROL

"As with Gladness Men of Old" (No. 196)

THE CONCLUSION

So the precious carols are meant to tell the Good News abroad in the spirit of joy and to inspire people everywhere to journey not just to Bethlehem but into life for the sake of the Gift given. It is hoped that the church will guard their sacredness, use them with understanding, and help the world to know the Savior they proclaim.

THE BENEDICTION AND CHORAL RESPONSE

THE POSTLUDE "Christmas Chorale" Deigendesch   □

Christmas Songs

Long Ago, There Was Born

P. W. Blackmer

Johannes Brahms, 1833-1897
Arr. by Nevin W. Fisher, b. 1900

1. Long a - go, there was born In the cit - y of Da - vid,
2. Je - sus came as a child From His Fa - ther in heav - en,

A sweet, ho - ly Babe, Who was Je - sus our King,
And has shown us the way To be lov - ing and kind,

An - gels sang at His birth, "Lull-a - by, peace on earth,"
While the stars sang a - bove, "Lull-a - by, God is love,"

An - gels sang at His birth, "Lull-a - by peace on earth."
While the stars sang a - bove, "Lull-a - by God is love."

Brightest and Best of the Sons of the Morning

Reginald Heber, 1783-1826, alt.

MORNING STAR 11.10.11.10.
James (John) P. Harding, ?-1911

1 Bright - est and best of the sons of the morn - ing,
2 Cold on his cra - dle the dew - drops are shin - ing,
3 Say, shall we yield him, in cost - ly de - vo - tion,
4 Vain - ly we of - fer each am - ple ob - la - tion;
5 Bright - est and best of the sons of the morn - ing,

Dawn on our dark - ness, and lend us thine aid;
Low lies his head with the beasts of the stall;
O - dors of E - dom and of - ferings di - vine,
Vain - ly with gifts would his fa - vor se - cure;
Dawn on our dark - ness, and lend us thine aid;

Star of the east, the ho - ri - zon a - dorn - ing,
An - gels a - dore him, in slum - ber re - clin - ing,
Gems of the moun - tain, and pearls of the o - cean,
Rich - er by far is the heart's ad - o - ra - tion,
Star of the east, the ho - ri - zon a - dorn - ing,

Guide where our in - fant Re - deem - er is laid!
Mak - er, and Mon - arch, and Sav - ior of all.
Myrrh from the for - est, or gold from the mine?
Dear - er to God are the prayers of the poor.
Guide where our in - fant Re - deem - er is laid! A - men.

"Sing of the Baby"

Oh we s-i-n-g of the ba-by, ba-by Je-sus

born to-day In a man-ger, in a man-ger,

far a-way, far a-way. O'er the man-ger,

O'er the man-ger in the sky a shi—ny star

Guides the wisemen to the ba-by in a man-ger

filled with hay. Sing! Sing! of the ba-by

in the man-ger far a-way. Sing! Sing!

of the ba-by. Born for us on Christ-mas day!

Sing Ye All Hosanna

Lyrics and music by Steve Engle

1. 'Twas a fros-ty win-ter morn when the Ho-ly Babe was born in a
2. Came three wise men from a-far, be-ing guid-ed by that star o-ver

man-ger so rough and bare._____ But the child was safe and warm.
Beth-le-hem it came to rest._____ There they found the Babe and knelt,

He was shel-tered from life's storm by the moth-er love____ kin-dled there.____ (No Chorus)
bear-ing gifts of pre-cious wealth: off'ring gold and myrrh and frank-in-cense.____

CHORUS

Sing ye all Ho-san-na. Sing Al-le-lu-ia!____ Glo-ry to

God, peace on earth, good will to men! Sing ye all Ho-san-na!____ Sing Al-le-

lu-ia!____ Glo-ry to God, peace on earth, good will to men.____ *Fine*

3. Vir-gin Ma-ry soft and mild, bend-ing o'er the sleep-ing child; Did she
4. Cen-tu-ries have now gone by since our glo-rious Sav-ior died And my

know the hymn the an-gels sang?____ And the joy he was to bring to a
broth-ers, if you're won-der-ing,____ In this sin-ful world of ours you can

world long suf-fer-ings: of peace and love____ to____ ev'ry land.____ (Repeat Chorus)
walk be-neath the stars, and if you lis-ten hear the an-gels sing:____